All you need to know about party throwing, party going, themes, surprises, social blunders, sexual overtures, name dropping, fancy dressing, drunken brawling, social climbing, gatecrashers, wallflowers, angry neighbours, dangerous dance steps, limp salads, paper plates, doctored punch, twist-cap wine, organised games, outstayed welcomes, making merry, feeling poorly, behaving badly and impossible tiny street maps on invitations that get read underneath lamp posts.

≈   ≈   ≈

The Ultimate Party Book

The Ultimate Party Book

THE ILLUSTRATED GUIDE TO SOCIAL INTERCOURSE

Christopher Fowler

Illustrated by
Stuart Buckley

London
UNWIN PAPERBACKS
Boston   Sydney

UNWIN® PAPERBACKS
40 Museum Street, London WC1A 1LU, UK

Unwin Paperbacks
Park Lane, Hemel Hempstead, Herts HP2 4TE, UK

George Allen & Unwin Australia Pty Ltd
8 Napier Street, North Sydney, NSW 2060, Australia

Unwin Paperbacks with the
Port Nicholson Press
PO Box 11–838 Wellington, New Zealand

First published by Unwin Paperbacks, 1985
Reprinted 1986

ISBN 0 04 793087 X

Set in 16 on 20 point Joanna by Nene Phototypesetters Ltd, Northampton
and printed in Great Britain by Hazell Watson and Viney Limited,
Member of the BPCC Group, Aylesbury, Bucks

Contents

1.

FEARS OF PARTY GOING & THROWING
'I mean,' he laughed, 'what could *possibly* go wrong?'

~ ~ ~

2.

MAKING AN ENTRANCE
Standing in front of the wardrobe for two hours saying you've nothing to wear, then arriving late.

~ ~ ~

3.

CHECKING OUT THE CROWD
Guest-spotting, gatecrashing and talking to mad people.

~ ~ ~

4.

PARTY FATE
You *know* it will happen before the night's out . . .

~ ~ ~

5.

PARTY MUSIC
Bad sounds and balding DJs.

~ ~ ~

6.

ATTACK OF THE FIFTY-FOOT BUFFET!
The hidden dangers of party food.

~ ~ ~

7.
SOUR GRAPES
Remembering to put the lid on the cocktail blender.

~   ~   ~

8.
IMPOSSIBLE TINY STREET MAPS THAT GET READ BENEATH LAMP POSTS
I told you we should have turned left at the crematorium.

~   ~   ~

9.
PARTY THEMES & GAMES
Men who dress up, and why. Games in which you can legitimately make someone cry.

~   ~   ~

10.
THE TOP TEN PARTY GUESTS OF ALL TIME
Make it eleven if you include yourself.

~   ~   ~

11.
SURPRISE!
The Horrible Truth about surprise parties.

~   ~   ~

12.
ALTERED STATES
The effects of party dr*gs, or What's Up Your Nose, Doc?

~   ~   ~

13.

THE OFFICE CHRISTMAS PARTY

What to do when the boss removes your glasses and says,
'Why, but you're *beautiful*!'

≈   ≈   ≈

14.

FIGHTING AT PARTIES

'Don't make a scene!' she hissed through clenched teeth.

≈   ≈   ≈

15.

THE PARTY QUIZ

The questions *Cosmopolitan* didn't dare ask.

≈   ≈   ≈

16.

OUTDOOR PARTIES

Picnics, fetes, scavenger hunts and five inches of rain.

≈   ≈   ≈

17.

THAT'S ENTERTAINMENT?

Party performers, and how to get them off the stage.

≈   ≈   ≈

18.

FUNCTIONAL DINNERS

Clip-on bow ties and the world's rudest waiters.

≈   ≈   ≈

19.

SEX AT PARTIES
'Whoops, sorry, I was just looking for my coat!'

≈ ≈ ≈

20.

JET SET PARTIES
Parking your bike between two Porsches
and pretending you're rich.

≈ ≈ ≈

21.

THE BEST & WORST PARTIES
Whether or not to invite Barry Manilow.

≈ ≈ ≈

22.

AFTER THE BOMB
Hangovers, clearing up, and who's that in the kitchen
wrapped in a bedspread making breakfast?

≈ ≈ ≈

Acknowledgements

Love and thanks to the party guests who posed for the pictures:

Margaret Armitage, always in the kitchen at parties (usually eating).

Bernard Briquet, who tells us that it's an old French custom to go home before the washing up.

Stuart Buckley, illustrious illustrator and the Warren Beatty of the party circuit.

'Boogaloo' Sue Collins, who knows that true partygoers bring their tapshoes.

Mike Devery, always in the bathroom at parties (and in his underpants at surprise ones).

Sarah Fforde, who brought charm and calm to a disgracefully rowdy crowd.

Andrew Hunt, who brought a touch of class to the proceedings (even in a dress).

Steve Hutchinson, who played with lit fireworks for us (get well soon, Steve!).

Deana Mash, a true lady, always removes a man's glasses before she hits him.

Victoria Plaistow, still searching for her contact lens in the carpet.

Roger Smith, our druggie, whose party exploits can be followed in the sort of magazines your newsagent slips inside an *Exchange & Mart* before selling to you.

Jim Sturgeon, whose neighbours enjoyed his garden barbeque party the next day by simply sniffing their washing.

Sally Talbot, the gal with the million dollar smile and the same taste in restaurants.

Special thanks to Tom, Chris, Fiona, Paul, Mark, Greg, Andy and Jackie, all of whom were prepared to pose until closing.

Thanks also to David 'Party Boy' Beckman and Eric, California's next biggest attraction after Disneyland, and to Kim Freitas (What is the secret of his incredible success?).

To Johnny and Francis, Ronnie and Marcia, Richard and Dina, Val and Martin, it's time you all threw parties.

Serafina, meet you in Kettners, whose champagne bar may be recommended to all discerning partygoers. Tell Lisa we sent you.

TO KATH AND BILL

Who until today were
unaware that I threw a party in
their lounge while they were
away, and completely
repainted it before they
returned.

Introduction

Pay close attention. This is a briefing session. I want you to know what you're letting yourself in for here. You see, everyone complains about having a good time. They complain about having to organise one, having to be present at one, seeing other people enjoying one, clearing up after one and not having as much of one as the next person.

This is because having a good time in the twentieth century requires much preparation and organisation. Yes, it would be nice to think that enjoyment – that is, real pleasure derived from a perfect mixture of people and surroundings – could be spontaneously stimulated in the course of everyday life. But of course, smart go-ahead people like you and me know that this is entirely impossible. We have only to look at the bargain basement rag-bag of mental case-histories we are forced to conduct transactions with on a daily basis to realise that there are several hundred species of leguminous tree more colourful and interesting than most of our colleagues.

The most common form of organised good time is The Party. This instantly gives everyone something to complain about, because nobody likes being told in advance how and when to enjoy themselves.

What you are doing when you decide to hold a party, is arranging to fill a room for several hours with a disparate group of aggressive, nervous, hypertense, overreactive and insular strangers whose only defence against a barrage of venom-laced party banter is to get so blasted that a cruise missile could come through the roof without so much as causing them to snap the stems of their wine glasses.

But don't let that worry you.

If you think of the doubts and fears that assail you from the moment you accept an invitation to the moment you walk into a room full of people, and multiply those fears by the number of people you've invited to your social gathering, you'll realise that there is no way you can provide everyone with the perfect evening.

The sooner you realise this, the sooner we can all start having fun. Honestly, if you're going to be difficult all through the book, you might as well go home, lock the doors and go to bed with the Raj Quartet.*

As for the rest of you, and here I am taking it for granted that I am addressing a group of gregarious, erudite, charming, life-affirming people who are always on the lookout for an evening which is going to be somewhat less than a total utter drag, what we plan to do here is to lay out the pleasures and pitfalls of satisfying, well-lubricated social intercourse.

We've discovered what makes a good party, and what dooms one, and we're going to share that knowledge with you.

But what, you say, qualifies us to preach to you, someone who is already worldly, hip, clued in and a pretty snappy dresser to boot.

Well, Stuart, the illustrator, and myself have recently

* The books, not the restaurant performers.

conducted an extensive series of heavily researched tests into the world of parties.

Stuart is eminently qualified to do this because in addition to being incredibly talented he is also witty, stylish, charming to a degree and possessing of a snake-and-mongoose type effect with the opposite sex which gains him admittance to the most exclusive parties in the world.

I am qualified because I go with him.

Our research has taken us from the smartest cocaine-and-cut-crystal cocktail parties of London and Los Angeles to the kind of miserable beer swilling evening that would make a night locked in a launderette with a pair of Jehovah's Witnesses seem like dinner at the Ritz.

What we have learned from these exhausting experiences is written and drawn on the following pages.

1. Fears of party going

What could possibly go wrong? It's just a few people! Nick will be there! Nick, who you haven't seen since college! And Maggie and Jeff *always* throw a terrific party! You'll have so much fun!

No, you won't, because when you get there you find that Jeff walked out on Maggie last night and she was unable to cancel the guests in time. She has apparently locked herself in the bedroom but says to Help Yourself To Anything and Have a Good Time. There used to be a photo montage of her and Jeff on the kitchen notice board, but someone seems to have torn it in half and stuffed it into the pedal bin. Nick from college hasn't turned up. In between record tracks you can hear muffled sobbing coming through the living room ceiling. You wish you'd stayed at home and scraped the oven out.

This is an extreme example of a terrible evening, but even so, approximately only one in every fifteen parties are any good at all.

No amount of Shavian wit at a party will make up for the fact that since ten thirty there has been just half a bottle of warm Blue Nun left in the kitchen. No amount of superb food will compensate for the fact that the host owns just four record albums, two of of which feature the flute hits of James Galway, 'Bossa Nova' style.

Even if all the other factors are favourable, the problem may simply lie in the bad casting of the guest list.

And if this sounds as if everything is conspiring

towards you having a lousy time, consider some of the things that could conceivably go wrong:

SITUATION A
~ ~ ~

You are a single male, recently jilted and badly in need of cheering up. Someone in the office invites you to a party on Saturday night. You eagerly accept the invitation. When you arrive at the house, you find that:

1. The place is in darkness. You reread the invitation and discover that the party is in two weeks' time. You took so long finding the house that it is now too late to go anywhere else.

2. You are the only person not dressed as a vicar or a schoolgirl.

3. The party consists entirely of middle-aged couples in evening wear, and the host asks you where your 'other half' is tonight.

4. The party consists entirely of overweight drunks playing cards who see parties as a chance to 'get away from the ball and chain and have fun'.

5. There are twenty-five elderly hippies sitting in a circle on the lounge floor drinking herbal tea and discussing Jack Kerouac.

6. The bouncy disco music lures you into a room containing thirty gay men and two fat girls.

7. You find you are inadvertently attending an EST seminar recruitment party

8. You find yourself standing in a room with 150

3. Within three minutes of arriving, an extremely obnoxious man latches on to you and follows you around for the rest of the evening.

4. Everyone in the whole place is stoned or drunk. You cannot get into the bathroom because someone has passed out in there with their back against the door.

5. The man who asked you to dance has been at the quiche all evening – which is loaded with garlic. He dances like an epileptic ostrich. The song is 'Bridge Over Troubled Water'. Everyone around you joins in on the chorus.

6. A man asks you to dance. You are tired, but accept graciously. The record is a long-playing disco version of an old song. Twenty-three minutes later it is still going strong. You can no longer feel your legs.

7. The men invite you over to hear the latest jokes someone just heard, involving two stewardesses and a rapist.

8. The lights are turned way down low when you arrive, everyone is necking and there is something fleshy and pulsing on the video which looks as if it might be part of the human body, upside down. You take your wine bottle to the kitchen and stay there.

9. Within five minutes of arriving, someone has managed to spill a glass of red wine over you. While you are sponging the stain out at the kitchen sink you notice the men behind you staring in disgust as if you were drunk.

10. It's a dinner party. You have just eaten.

11. It's a drinks party. You are starving, and spend the evening overdosing on cheese puffs.

12. Your arrival goes unnoticed, as everyone is in the kitchen trying to stop a fight.

13. Upon your arrival, the first thing someone says to you is, 'You just missed all the fun.'

14. The party is attended by your ex-fiancé and his new male lover.

15. The lights are out when you ring the front doorbell. It transpires that the party is a surprise one, and the dozens of Polaroid flashbulbs that burst at your entry signify that you have just been mistaken for the person whose birthday it actually is. In the ensuing clear-up of mistaken identity, the real birthday guest arrives unheralded.

16. Nearly everyone has brought children. Right now there are six little boys running in a circle around the adults screaming, two little girls trying to get the lid up on the piano, and a very small child sitting with its legs straight out in front of it screaming 'POTTY!' to anyone who will take notice.

FEARS OF PARTY THROWING
~ ~ ~

The flipside of these depressing possibilities is actually worse. At least you can leave an awful party. When you're throwing one, there's no escape. Of course, a number of factors can be determined by you to reduce the possibility of ghastly goings-on . . . food, drink, music, ambience, keeping cat hairs out of the cocktail onions, and so on.

Your biggest risk element is in the motley crowd you so hastily invited at the last minute, and the possibility that they will all have a terrible time, or worse still, such a great time that they completely demolish your home in doing so.

You should be aware that one of the following five desperate situations could very easily develop. Still, it's better to get these potential problems out in the open so that you'll be able to recognise them should one start to arise at your party. After all, you know what they say . . . a worry shared is two people worried.

SITUATION 1
~ ~ ~

It is nine thirty. The garlic bread came out of the oven too early, and now sits cooling on the kitchen counter along with the rapidly de-chilling wine. The room is empty except for two people who arrived at eight. You keep telling them that any moment now the room will become packed with guests. They appear unconvinced, and from time to time glance furtively toward their coats. IT IS IMPERATIVE that they are not allowed to leave before your other guests arrive, for if they do, they will be convinced for evermore that you have no friends, and will never again attend one of your parties.

SITUATION 2
~ ~ ~

It is ten o'clock and NOBODY AT ALL has arrived. You're sure you know where they are, they're all in the pub, but if you leave to fetch them they will suddenly turn up here, and finding nobody at home, will curse you and head off somewhere else. Either that, or by some incredible twist of fate nobody could make it at the last

7

minute and they all lost your phone number and couldn't phone, leaving you sitting here changing records and folding the paper napkins into swans.

SITUATION 3
~ ~ ~

So far the only people to arrive – about eight of them – are the people you least know and/or like but felt compelled to invite as they would have found out about the party anyway. The only other person to arrive so far is someone you admire enormously and seek to impress. That person has been collared by the most boring of the other guests, and is even now revising his opinion of you. There is nothing you can say or do which will not make matters worse.

SITUATION 4
~ ~ ~

A few minutes after the party has really begun to pick up, your mother arrives unannounced. Peering around the door she says, 'Oh, you've got People in. Well, I won't stop. I don't want to spoil the good time you're having with your friends.' She says this in a manner which fills you with guilt and compels you to invite her in. When you return from the kitchen with her drink, you find her sitting on the couch discussing hosiery with Divine, who was performing in town and arrived with a friend. From time to time she looks over at you with her eyes narrowed.

SITUATION 5
~ ~ ~

You have planned a small drinks party, primarily for some of the people with whom you do business. Your

8

most important client has promised to put in an appearance. You figure that the party will run from seven until ten, with good wine, simple hors d'oeuvres, pleasing conversation and perhaps a couple of useful business connections made. Out of politeness, you have invited two of your regular drinking buddies along.

These two arrive early bearing party cans of beer. One of them says he hopes you don't mind, but as he was meeting some friends he invited them to call in.

The 'friends' who call in include:

A seven-foot tall black guy on roller skates carrying a ghetto blaster.

A loud drunken woman whose shoulderstraps have fallen down.

An angry-looking 17-year-old with a tangerine Mohawk and a nail through his nose who opens beer bottles with his teeth.

Another angry-looking kid with a spider-web tattooed across his forehead who keeps shouting 'OI OI OI' and jumping up and down on the spot.

A stoned art student who keeps trying to stick joints in your bank manager's mouth while he explains how he would overthrow capitalistic institutions using his policy of 'Ultra-aggressive Anarchy'.

It boils down to the fact that whether you're throwing a party or merely planning to attend one, your misgivings are well founded. There are thousands of ways, as yet undreamt of, for perfect strangers to humiliate and embarrass you at social gatherings.

At this stage, therefore, it is important to develop a mental survival kit which will see you through the most horrible of evenings. This does not mean you have to carry a set of jump leads in an evening bag. It means that you should be prepared to shine on through any eventuality. In chapters ahead, I'll show you just how to do this, what to avoid, what to look for, and where they hide it when there are people about.

2. Making an entrance

This has nothing to do with home improvements, any more than it has to do with arriving in a silver-sequined boob tube and firing a marine flare every time you wish to make a statement.

Let's assume that, on occasion, you are prepared to be reasonably extrovert in your appearance and behaviour, and that the party you are about to attend will draw out the innate sense of spirited good humour you had all the time before you were married.

What should you wear? When should you arrive? What should you bring?

In these matters I seek not to dictate, but merely to advise and point out a few of the Awful Mistakes you could make.

There is a slim chance that you will not agree with the opinions expressed in the following chapters, in which case you probably have the dress sense of a Patagonian Blue Mandrill and are beneath the attention of all save those in the insect world.

FASHION HELL
~ ~ ~

Your guide to avoiding Fashion Hell, where tortured victims are forced to wear pale green flared slacks with brown elastic-sided shoes and mauve nylon shirts for eternity, lies in your knowledge of the hostess or host, the time of the event, the venue and who else is liable to be there.

Beware of overdressing in daylight hours unless the occasion is very special. Then again, if you dress down, and arrive to find everyone else looking their very best, you'll feel a complete scruffbag.

Of course, you may naturally *be* a totally revolting, lice-teeming scruffbag, in which case kindly replace this book on the shelf, wipe the smears from the cover and move on. Your place is in the Harold Robbins section.

If you are male, and attending an evening dress function, try to avoid the 'rented shiny-bottomed tux' look that most men plonk for. White cotton jackets are great if you want people to think you work for Mr Whippy.

If you are female, try to avoid the 'Low-Cut Off-The-Shoulder All-Purpose Party-Dress' look common to such functions. Also, beware of wrap-around evening dresses at drafty garden parties unless you look good standing with a glass of wine in one hand and your dress over your head.

Ladies who attend functions in outfits that look terrific on *Vogue* models twenty years younger than themselves are generally laughed at, although I personally feel that a woman who attends a vicarage fete wearing a backless gold lamé gown with the front cut to below sea level certainly brightens up the afternoon, especially if she enters the egg and spoon race.

At a casual drinks party in the home, there is a tendency for married men to turn up in baggy, snagged Fair Isle sweaters with beer-stained leather elbow patches and strands of pipe tobacco down the front. While such attire has not actually brought about the collapse of civilisation's social structure, it does anger the Fashion

... standing with a glass of wine
in one hand and your dress
over your head.

13

Gods, and it depresses your fellow guests to think that your life is comfortable enough for you not to have to worry about how you dress.

One other thing. There is a rumour going around that not wearing any socks makes you look rich. It does not. It makes you look as if you should be sitting in a launderette waiting for the rinse cycle to end. There remain the following Party Dress Rules:

PARTY DRESS RULES
~ ~ ~

* ★ KAFTANS DO NOT FLATTER FAT PEOPLE (Remember Demis Roussos?)
* ★ ANY MAN WITH MORE THAN HIS TOP THREE SHIRT BUTTONS OPEN IS A HAIRDRESSER.
* ★ GIRLS IN LEGWARMERS HAD BETTER BE ABLE TO DANCE.
* ★ CHARM BRACELETS BELONG ON GYPSY FORTUNE-TELLERS.
* ★ SOME WOMEN AGE ELEGANTLY. OTHERS WEAR DESIGNER JEANS.
* ★ NEVER SPEAK TO PEOPLE WHO LOOK LESS INTERESTING THAN THEIR HAIRSTYLES.
* ★ CLOTHES WITH BIG DESIGNER LABELS ARE FINE IF YOU WISH TO LOOK LIKE A BILLBOARD.

~ ~ ~

But enough about fashion. Theoretically, people are more interested in finding out about you than your clothes.

Which is fine until you spend twenty minutes explaining your stance on the current political situation to someone, only to have them ask you where you bought your shoes.

TIMING YOUR ARRIVAL
~ ~ ~

Having accepted an invitation to a party, the first mistake you can make is in arriving too early. It used to be almost impossible to arrive too late. But in these less decadent times punctuality is considered a mark of style and self-control.

Dinner parties require prompt arrival as a matter of course. It is no longer considered amusing to arrive at a society sit-down halfway through the Poulet Katchaturian pissed out of one's mind.

At a stand-up function, the ideal arrival point is one half-hour after the time stated on the invitation. That is to say, when the main room is partly filled with guests.

Early arrival implies that the hard blank white of the pages in your social diary is enough to cause mild snow blindness, and that this is the first time you have been out of the house in years.

Late arrival implies that the 'EVENING' portions of your appointments calendar are so crammed with pencilled social obligations that the only reason you are deigning to attend tonight is because your secretary couldn't find an eraser.

Regardless of what time you arrived, you must NEVER EVER be the first person to leave unless you have an excellent excuse for doing so, such as only having a few hours left to live. Social intercourse is as any other: Timing is Essential.

WHAT TO TAKE WITH YOU

~ ~ ~

There was a time when you could stick a bottle of Australian burgundy on the kitchen counter as you walked through and nobody batted an eyelid.

Nowadays, thanks to the advent of winebars and cocktail bars all called 'Gatsby's' and 'Corks' everyone is a self-styled drinks expert, and caution must be exercised when selecting a party bottle. Choose something you yourself would be prepared to drink, and remember that it's nearly always the dry white wine that runs out first at a party.

Arriving with a bottle of vodka is vulgar, and makes you look like a lush. Arriving with a bottle of Slivovitch in the shape of a bell, containing a sprayed-gold plastic ballerina which spins around to the tune of the Anniversary Waltz when you set the bottle down (something I actually received at a party) makes you look a complete loony, but it does guarantee that the bottle will still be there unopened at the end of the evening. In fact, it was still there unopened on the kitchen counter three years later when I moved apartments (I told the new renters it came with the lease).

A small thoughtfully chosen gift makes an excellent alternative to the usual bottle. How about a plant or a book? How about this book? How about ten copies?

GIFTS NOT TO TAKE TO PARTIES

~ ~ ~

★ A Willy Warmer

- ★ Anything sex shops sell as jokes, like condoms with ears
- ★ An ice cube tray which makes ice in the shape of breasts
- ★ Joke books about bodily functions, Terry Wogan or other impolite subjects
- ★ An ant farm
- ★ Plastic Bar-B-Q aprons printed with the words 'I'M THE BOSS!'
- ★ Anything Snoopy or Garfield
- ★ Toilet paper with crossword puzzles on

BUT WAIT A MINUTE! . . .

~ ~ ~

I hear you cry.

The world is trembling on the brink of an apocalypse and here you are wanting me to worry about whether it is socially acceptable to arrive at a smart soirée bearing a smutty card and a 'funny' latex willy. How can I, a concerned right-thinking responsible citizen be bothered with such tawdry transient pleasures?

Good point. With the world in the state it's in, should we really be concerned with such trivial matters? You bet. I say, worry about all the crackers that go damp waiting to be eaten on buffet tables and the Really Important Stuff that's happening globally will be decided for you.

Come to think of it, it will be even if you don't give a toss about overmoist party edibles. But just to put your mind at ease . . .

HOW A NUCLEAR HOLOCAUST COULD AFFECT YOUR DINNER PARTY
~ ~ ~

1. You would not need to reheat food in the microwave prior to serving.

2. You would not need to light the dining table candles, as guests will be providing their own illumination.

3. The inside of your steak will not be undercooked.

4. Boring dinner conversation will be drowned out by a deafening bang.

5. Hairs found in the food will be from guests' own heads.

6. Embarrassing conversational faux pas will be eclipsed by events demanding greater attention i.e. windows being blown in, roof flying off, etc.

7. Steak more of a problem to enjoy owing to sudden absence of guests' teeth.

8. Red wine stains on Irish linen tablecloth obscured by tons of rubble.

9. No arguments over who will do the washing up.

10. No need to worry about return invitations.

3. Checking out the crowd

Before the hostess takes one look at you standing in the doorway, mentally labels you a minor star in her invited constellation and steers you towards a corner containing a group of similar untouchables whose conversation is bound to be irrepressibly drab and awful, take time out to see who's here and plot your own course through the room.

A quick 360 of the surrounding area should reveal a few people you would be prepared to hold a conversation with – and a few you should avoid at all costs . . .

GUEST SPOTTING AT A GLANCE

~ ~ ~

1. The sour-looking woman in the maroon Laura Ashley dress drinking an orange juice is the wife of someone who has been neglecting her all night. She is bitter and conversationally weird. She is also carefully staying sober so that, later, she can hiss 'You're drunk!' in a disgusted manner to her husband in the car.

2. Spot the gay man. Check his socks. All gay men wear white socks. Also, gay men only wear one type of jeans: straight-legged boot-cut 501's. Now that all gay men look like weightlifters and lumberjacks, these are your only sure signs.

3. Avoid the Loudmouth. He is the husband of the woman drinking fruit juice, but he's trying to pretend he's still single. He's wearing gold chains and refers to his wrist-watch as a 'digital chronometer'. He tells dirty jokes

19

Labelling your guests at a glance ...

20

to women and tries to arrange to meet them later in the week. In his efforts to appear under 30 he uses bronzer and wears bikini underwear.

4. There is an even louder, overweight drunk in the centre of the room talking to a group of people. He takes large gulps from a vodka and tonic between sentences. The words 'airdate', 'tape transfer' and 'production budget' may be discerned in his conversation. Avoid this man. He is a television producer, and as such is prepared to do anything at all to you or your family short of actually eating your children.

5. The tall, scarecrow thin woman chattering and waving her arms about is also one to avoid. The frightening intensity in her eyes should warn you that here is a manic depressive walking a highly greased emotional tightrope. Every now and again she lets out a piercing, high pitched laugh that sounds like a bird being killed and makes everyone in the room stop talking and look up at the ceiling. High likelihood of a hysterical fit/major crying jag in the bathroom before the end of the evening.

6. There is an emaciated sinister-looking man in a black satin jacket standing alone at the buffet. He looks unwell, as if he has had too many late nights for too long. He has no friends. The back of his jacket reads:

MOTORHEAD SUMMER TOUR '83

Do not feel sorry for this man! He is a record executive, which is to say he is as near as you can get to a human being without actually being one. He is prepared to lie, cheat and steal for no reason beyond the twisted pleasure it affords him. He cannot help this, and genuinely does not understand why people treat him as they would nuclear waste or any other toxic substance.

Having spotted the group above, your best bet is to go and talk to the gay man. He will compliment your choice of clothes, offer you a drink and ask you to dance whether you are male or female.

To the trained eye, most truly awful party types may be detected by their manner and can be easily avoided. Some, however, have the ability to camouflage themselves quite effectively, and do not reveal their true colours until you, poor innocent, have been snared in their trap. And a trap it is, for these are people whose only successful method of finding a dance partner is to dig a pit, cover it with leaves and wait for someone to fall in.

Here, in an easy to follow chart, are the major types.

MAJOR PARTY TYPES: WHAT TO LOOK FOR
~ ~ ~

SEX	NAME	DRESS	OPENING LINE	CHOSEN CONVERSATION TOPIC	OUTCOME
Male	Brian	Grey suit, tie with little tennis racquets on. Tassled loafers.	'I don't know anyone here except the hostess, do you?'	Similar party he went to where he didn't know anyone there, either.	Will ask you if you'd like a refill, then will forget all about it and carry on talking.
Female	Deidre	Maroon Laura Ashley dress with high collar. Boots.	'I hate parties, don't you?'	Similar parties which she has also hated.	Will stare silently into her drink until you leave.

SEX	NAME	DRESS	OPENING LINE	CHOSEN CONVERSATION TOPIC	OUTCOME
Male	Wayne	Jeans, T-shirt bearing Playboy bunny symbol.	'Have you seen that girl with the massive tits?'	Absence of girls at parties these days with massive tits.	Will stumble off to proposition all girls in room and be amazed to hear his suggestions rejected.
Female	Cheryl	Tight, low-cut Disco top, stretch jeans, 3 inch heels.	'That guy in the Playboy T-shirt won't leave me alone.'	Men who won't leave her alone at parties.	Will ask you back to her place.
Male	Nigel	Corduroy jacket, suede shoes with argyle socks, club tie.	Nasal whine renders first line indistinct: Something about what you do for a living.	What he does, who his father is, and how many 'old' connections his family have.	Will continue to talk to you as if you are a stray dog for as long as you stand there.
Female	Gemma	Dressed like Business Class air hostess.	'I wonder how she gets her crevettes to stay on top of her vol-au-vents?'	Booker Prize shortlistings, TV show 'Dynasty', house-hunting, difficulties of.	Conversation ends when you discover that her husband is your boss.
Female	Jane	Save The Whales T-shirt, fringed jeans & backpack.	'How do you justify working in (say, advertising) when millions of seals are being butchered?'	Plight of the Patagonian Blue Mandrill.	You tell her you justify your job by using salary to buy food. Conversation takes an immediate dive from there.
Male	Arthur	Cardigan, no jacket, thick glasses.	'I do ballroom dancing, you know.'	Comparative ballroom dancing championship performances for the years 1935 to the present day.	You will go to the toilet and not come back.
Male	Sven	Jeans, T-shirt, orange nylon backpack.	Doesn't seem to speak English. Sounds like the cook on The Muppet Show.	Asks in broken English if you have seen show 'Evita', tells you he is foreign exchange student but does not say what we sent his country in return.	Wanders off to sit on backpack in corner and spends rest of evening writing in diary.

SEX	NAME	DRESS	OPENING LINE	CHOSEN CONVERSATION TOPIC	OUTCOME
Female	Sally	Jeans, sweater.	Polite demurrance to your offer of drink, food, dance, sharing rest of your life, etc.	Limited to a few 'Hmm's' with the odd nod and shake of the head where the conversation demands it. Looks away a lot.	Shows visible relief as huge boyfriend returns and gives you a look which could crack a stack of roofing tiles.
Female	Stephanie	Tightest jeans in the world, tiny boob tube.	'You shouldn't eat that. Anything over seventy calories an ounce causes heart disease.'	Dieting, depression at being fat (this despite the fact that she weighs about five stone) difficulty of managing curly hair, teenage rock stars, how she deals with hypertension.	Will burst into tears for no reason at all and spend rest of evening telephoning her ex-boyfriend.
Male	Howard	T-shirt with Captain Marvel on front. Sandals with black socks. Whispy beard.	'Who's your favourite science fiction writer? Wonder if they've got any Hawkwind?'	Role playing games, comics, fantasy films. 'Star Trek', societies that track down UFO's, reincarnation, spacemen.	Will go into the garden to take drugs and see if he can spot the space vehicles that we on earth have named Ursa Major.
Female	Ray (née Charlotte)	Dirty jeans, smock, sandals.	'What are all these men doing here? I thought it was going to be women only.'	Men, hatred and sufferance of. Women, subjugation and domination of by men. Town Council, refusal of to set up lesbian community surrounded by moat and drawbridge.	Any light-heartedness you were feeling earlier will be crushed to death by ponderance of lecture. You fall asleep.
Male	David	Check shirt, 501's, boots, moustache, cropped black hair, Rolex Oyster.	'Isn't this the 12″ Remix of an old Gloria Gaynor song?'	Discos, Black American female singers, opera, Piaget, Giorgio Armani, Van Kleef & Arpels, Bette Midler's last concert.	(If female) he will ask if you'd like to dance. (If male) he will ask you if you'd like to get married.

PARTY CONVERSATION

~ ~ ~

While I have every confidence in your ability to string a few amiable sentences together in the form of party small-talk, I cannot vouch for others, and must warn you that at some point in the evening you may be trapped in a corner listening to the rambling diatribe of someone who turns out to be completely mad. You can weed out the seriously unbalanced, however, by listening to their opening conversation. Getting away after this will prove the toughest part.

SPOTTING MAD OR BORING PEOPLE BY THEIR CONVERSATION

~ ~ ~

CONVERSATION TOPIC:	INDICATES PERSON IS:	AND WILL TRY TO:
Ideal Home Exhibition	Anal-retentive DIY freak	Tell you how to make pine bedroom furniture.
Expensive restaurants	Gold-digging freeloader	Wangle dinner invitation and use of your credit cards.
Reaching inner peace and self-realisation	Immature wreck who has now joined 'orange people'	Convince you that life will be freer once you have given away your car and stereo.
Visits to earth by other life forms	Mad	Stab you with cheese knife if you laugh.
Twelfth-century Flemish literature	Desperately lonely	Get into heated description of author you have never heard of.
Weird sex stuff	Potential News Of The World headliner	Drug your wine and do awful things while you sleep.
His most recent role	An actor	Talk about himself without stopping until dawn.
Hatred of 'lefties', 'arty' types, intellectuals etc.	On the police force	Get your home address by reading your library card upside down when you get a cigarette out.

HOW TO GET RID OF A MAD OR BORING PERSON AT A PARTY

~ ~ ~

Come on! Are you going to take this sort of bullying at a time when you should be enjoying yourself? No! The next time you get trapped by someone like this, here's what you tell them:

Well, funny you should say that because I phoned in to the BBC on the same topic at three this morning – I phone in to every show, all the time – but the pips went before I got through and I got very upset and burned one of my dolls – I always do that when I'm having an anxiety attack because the doctor at the institution told me it would help, not that it will ever cure my herpes, which always seems to be in its infectious stage these days, but at least it stops me going to the police about the men that come into my room at night and steal my toothpaste, although I'd like to see them try now because I've bought tons of toothpaste . . .

GATECRASHER SPOTTING

~ ~ ~

Whether you are throwing or just attending a party, gatecrashers are easy to spot in a crowd if you know what to look for. Keep an eye out for these tell-tale signs that reveal the amateurs:

1. A face full of food. The amateur crasher only gets to eat a couple of times a week. Watch for the stick of celery in the back pocket, the overloaded paper plate, the anaconda-like jaws that could expand to swallow half a loaf of French bread sideways in seconds.

2. Effort to look inconspicuous fails entirely owing to gatecrasher being inappropriately dressed in too-short trousers, weird, dated-looking shirt with huge collar, cravat and button advertising the show 'STARLIGHT EXPRESS'.

3. Hunted-looking, twitching eyes. The amateur crasher is always on the defensive. He expects to be challenged, and has an answer ready. The chances are that no one will challenge him. No one will even talk to him. He'll probably stay for half an hour then go home completely shattered that he was not able to tell anyone that he'd been invited by the host's ex-flatmate's sister.

CORRECT CRASHING
~ ~ ~

To those in the know there is a right way to crash a bash.

1. Wear a bow tie.

2. Act as if you own the place.

3. Introduce yourself to anyone standing alone. Tell them it's your party.

4. Smile a lot (very disarming, this). Throw back your head and laugh occasionally.

5. If anyone challenges you, tell them you're glad they could make it to your party and are they having a nice time? If it turns out that you're talking to the real host, brazen it out. Tell them it's a fabulous party and can you get them a glass of something? If your effrontery fails to take their breath away, offer to sleep with them.

6. Stand near a group of people, nodding and smiling. One of the group will think you know someone else there and treat you as a friend.

7. Spill a small amount of white wine over the person next to you. Apologise profusely and offer them a handkerchief. Point out that it's not easy being blind. Have them lead you around for the rest of the evening.

8. Be very casual refilling your glass and plate. The amateur crasher grips his glass as if it were the safety bar on a roller coaster.

9. If you decide to crash a wake, remember you can eat and drink as much as you like, but never start handing out business cards.

4. Party Fate

The time has come to speak plainly. Look, there are some things which always happen at parties, and they just happen and there's nothing you can do about them, so you must just put it down to Party Fate and accept them as they happen. And you know they will.

AT A PARTY YOU ARE THROWING . . .

1. You are convinced that you are not spending enough time with each of your guests. In your effort to be the perfect host and talk to everyone you will fail to have one single complete conversation with anyone and consequently your guests will think you are on drugs.

2. There are lots of people you must talk to tonight, but you won't get the chance, because someone you hardly know has trapped you in a corner and is asking you to describe in great detail exactly what it is you do for a living.

3. The longest ten seconds of your life will occur tonight when you forget the names of a couple you were introduced to minutes ago, while introducing them to a newly arrived guest.

4. At exactly 11.47 pm you will remember that there are three sticks of garlic bread still in the oven. They have been in there for five hours. Do not open the oven door under any circumstances.

5. At some point in the evening you will make a spectacular social gaffe, so try to get it over and done with

29

as early as possible. I have this theory that if you offer a medium-sized social blunder to the Conversation Gods, they will be appeased for the rest of the evening. Try something like this:

YOU:

~ ~ ~

'It's nice to see Jeffrey out without his boring, toad-faced, dull-witted, slow-moving, stunted dinosaur-like wife for once. Who are you, his mistress?'

HER:

~ ~ ~

'No, his wife's sister.'

6. Half an hour after the guests were supposed to arrive you experience a small nasty moment when you become convinced that you put your old telephone number on the invitations and nobody could call you to say that they couldn't come.

7. Having spent two whole days preparing the food, you will completely lose your appetite when the party starts and get drunk on two glasses of wine.

8. At exactly 11.48 pm the drink will run out and you are not sure that the party has sufficient energy to survive the wait while somebody runs over to their house for some more. While you are deciding what to do, new guests arrive.

9. Just before the evening arrivals begin, an involved and expensive item of clothing you are wearing comes undone, and you cannot work out how to do it up again without the diagram, which you threw away.

An involved and expensive item of clothing comes undone …

31

10. Just as the first guest asks, 'Where shall I put my coat?' you remember that the beds aren't made.

AT A PARTY YOU ARE ATTENDING . . .
≈　≈　≈

1. You will be forced to interrupt the conversation of the hostess to ask where she keeps the dustpan.

2. Despite the number of people who have used the bathroom all night, it is only after *you* have used it that the toilet won't stop flushing.

3. Unless they are hiding it in the attic, you notice that the unusual plant holder you bought your hosts last Christmas is nowhere in the house. Do not ask them about it or they will be forced to lie to you and say it got broken.

4. You will run into someone you haven't seen for ages and swear that you'll call them for lunch next week. They say that's what you said last time. You promise faithfully that you won't forget this time and *even as you are saying this you know you won't* because why else do you feel guilty already?

5. All evening long this person has been sitting alone on the other side of the room and you are convinced that you've met before. Finally you find yourselves standing next to each other in the kitchen, and the conversation goes like this:

YOU:
≈　≈　≈

'Excuse me, but your face is so familiar. Haven't we met somewhere before?'

32

OTHER PERSON:
~ ~ ~

'Yes. We slept together three and a half years ago. You never called.'

You remember nothing. They remember your name, address, occupation, favourite author and the colour of your bathroom.

6. You will mistake this guy for someone entirely different, only you won't realise it until ten minutes after you have parted. You will recall that throughout your conversation he gamely attempted to follow what you were saying with a look of puzzled amusement.

7. Any attempt to open a bottle of wine suavely in front of guests patiently holding empty glasses will result in your breaking the cork off halfway out of the bottle.

5. Party music

There are certain kinds of parties, those 'Let's-get-a-crowd-of-friends-together-and-all-get-drunk-won't-that-be-fun' type parties, that you will want to avoid from the start, because you know that the host will jealously guard the stereo all evening and only play old Led Zeppelin albums from the seventies interspersed with the kind of Heavy Metal band albums that have spotty Swedish foreign exchange students swaying about in Soho dive-bars in between their visits to see 'Evita'.

Music can transform the mood of a party to one of such profound melancholy that the people attending will consider heading to the bathroom with a large gin and a razor blade. Equally, good music can save a bad party – but there is a worrying trend afoot. Word has reached myself and fellow party researcher Stuart that there are people out there purchasing Barry Manilow albums and saving them exclusively for playing at parties. This is a sick and dangerous thing to do, and has led in the past to Guyana-style suicide pacts of immense proportions.

The people behind this are the self-same people who come to your house, pick up a rare and valuable album from your collection, and while they uncomprehendingly stare at the liner notes asking 'Do you actually *like* this kind of stuff?' let the record roll out of one side of the sleeve on to the floor.

Their own record collections consist of recent TV advertised 'Chart Topper' compilation albums and a battered old copy of 'Nat King Cole Sings Christmas Favourites'.

A cross-section of the Bad Host/ess's record collection will always look like this:

THE BAD HOST/ESS'S RECORD COLLECTION

ROLLER BOOGIE DOWN! (TV advertised chart hit album from 1979)

THE BOSTON POPS PLAY SONGS FROM 'HAIR' BOSSA NOVA STYLE

'EVITA' (Original Swedish cast)

THE THEME FROM 'GRANDSTAND' AND OTHER BBC SPORTS THEMES

THE THREE DEGREES SING DISCO VERSIONS OF THE SONGS FROM 'WEST SIDE STORY'

'BIRD ON THE WIRE' – LEONARD COHEN

NEAL HEFTI ARRANGES THE HITS OF CONNIE FRANCIS IN 'CHA CHA' SWINGTIME!

'633 SQUADRON' (Original soundtrack)

BARRY MANILOW'S GREATEST HITS

SPARKY'S MAGIC PIANO & TUBBY THE TUBA

'SATURDAY NIGHT FEVER' (Original soundtrack)

'THE MAGNIFICENT SEVEN' (Original soundtrack)

BBC RADIOPHONIC WORKSHOP SOUND EFFECTS RECORD – HORROR

THE BEST OF DEMIS ROUSSOS

'THE STUDENT PRINCE' – MARIO LANZA

'ERNIE THE MILKMAN & OTHER BAWDY FAVOURITES' – BENNY HILL

BERT KAEMPFERT'S SWINGIN' SAFARI!
ANNE MURRAY SINGS SONGS FROM 'DARK SIDE
OF THE MOON'
THE NORTH KOREAN FLUGELHORN ENSEMBLE
PERFORM 'JESUS CHRIST SUPERSTAR'
'RIDE A WHITE SWAN' – MARC BOLAN
(Scratched single)
THE SMURF'S CHRISTMAS ALBUM
'IN THE SUMMERTIME' – MUNGO JERRY
(Single, centre missing)
JANE FONDA'S WORKOUT ALBUM
'THE SOUND OF MUSIC' – (Not the original, but a cover
version performed by Bruce Forsyth and Dorothy Squires)
FRANK SINATRA LIVE AT CAESAR'S PALACE (Unplayable
since host's father became over emotional during
'STRANGERS IN THE NIGHT' and spilt Malibu and Coke
all over the turntable)
Y VIVA ESPANA! AND OTHER HOLIDAY SINGALONG
FAVOURITES
'BRIDGE OVER TROUBLED WATER' (Cover version of
album by two unknown Northern pub entertainers)
ELVIS – IN BETWEEN THE 'IN BETWEEN' YEARS
BOOTLEG BASEMENT TAPES VOL IV
K-TEL'S 500 GREATEST COUNTRY N' WESTERN
SMOOCHIES
BARRY WHITE AND THE LOVE UNLIMITED
ORCHESTRA PERFORM HEAVY METAL HEADBANGER
HITS

All I can suggest, faced with the vinyl dross in this little lot, is to start drinking heavily and encourage a singalong beginning 'A thousand green bottles hanging on a wall'.

If you're the one throwing the party, remember that it's easier to play cassettes as long as you rewind them, label them, and don't play the best ones first.

Hiring a DJ for the evening solves the problem of looking after the music, but creates a few new ones of its own . . .

THE DJ AND THE TURNTABLE OF DOOM
~ ~ ~

Unless you plan to employ a personal friend to DJ at your party, be very careful. Check out the credentials before hiring. Women DJs are generally pretty good. They mix music very well and are reasonably understanding when you ask if they have that record which goes 'Daa-do-do-WAA-WAA' in the middle.

On the other hand, BEWARE middle-aged white guys with their hair combed over the bald patch who shout 'YEAH! GET DOWN!' in the middle of records. These DJs are ex-cruise ship and Spanish hotel disco DJs who are bitter about not having their own radio show by now. For some reason, virtually all DJs are physically charmless and appear to have ordered their clothes over the phone from catalogues and discount warehouses. But this does not stop them from behaving like 14-year-old background dancers from TV disco programmes.

If you take the rash step of hiring a DJ for the evening without investigating him/her carefully first, you can guarantee that they will do some or all of the following things.

THE BAD DJ GUIDE
~ ~ ~

The DJ you have hired will:

1. Scream 'WHOOOOO-EEEEEEEEE!' in the middle of a record.

2. Shout 'ARE YOU HAVING A GOOD TIME?' and turn a deaf ear to the cries of 'NO!' that follow.

3. Mix records with five second gaps of complete silence between them.

4. Ask who's having a birthday or anniversary in the middle of your favourite track.

5. Dance around like an overweight John Travolta while the record is playing and knock the turntable so that it skips.

6. Say 'Sorry, never heard of it!' when you ask him to play the current No. 1.

7. Say 'Sorry, must have left it at home!' when you ask him for anything else.

8. Play 'Hi Ho Silver Lining' and turn the 'Hi Ho' bit down to get everyone to sing along.

9. Do the same thing with 'Hey You Get Off Of My Cloud' and encourage people to imitate Mick Jagger.

10. Play Spanish holiday singalong singles and get everyone to do the actions to the words.

11. Put on a twenty-minute long disco mix while he goes to the toilet and grabs a sandwich.

12. Be in the middle of pouring himself a drink in the kitchen when the record suddenly ends.

13. Become aggressive when you complain that his advertised 'Space Age Ultra-Tech Disco Mega-Lighting'

... plays 'Hi Ho Silver Lining' and
gets everyone to sing along.

39

consists of a red, blue and yellow light bulb on a stick.

14. Attempt to sexually assault the first attractive woman who passes in the mistaken assumption that she finds gold chains over a drip-dry nylon shirt and a lacquered Arthur Scargill hairdo a really big turn-on.

Unless you can absolutely guarantee that your DJ will do none of these things, stick to arranging your own music.

WHAT NOISE ANNOYS A NEIGHBOUR MOST?

Try Frankie Goes to Hollywood. That should do it. Before the party starts, it is a good idea to stick a note in the letterbox of your immediate neighbour which reads something like this.

Dear .... (Get name from bell)

I shall be having a party on the night of ....
which I am expecting quite a few friends to attend. We shall endeavour to keep the noise within acceptable boundaries, but should you find the music disturbing you, please do not hesitate to call me on this number
....

Kindest regards,

....

This is an excellent ploy, and the neighbours will be so amazed at your politeness that they'll probably leave you in peace. Do not attempt the more roughshod

40

approach below just because you are not on speaking terms with 'them next door'.

Dear Pustule Face,

After your last little shindig, which I seem to remember ended with the revolting sight of your common-law wife being sick out of an upstairs window just as the police arrived, this is to inform you that we will be staging a retaliatory knees-up that will make the Alamo look like a church picnic. If you don't want the vibrations from the old Sex Pistols albums we plan to play shaking every filling in your skull loose until seven in the morning, I tactfully suggest that you move to another city for the night.

Yours etc.,

....

6. Attack of the fifty foot buffet!

THE HIDDEN DANGERS OF PARTY FOOD

~ ~ ~

Parties bring out the Mr and Ms Hyde in their throwers. Their eyes light up at the thought of a roomful of starving guests being forced to consume the results of their experiments.

Yellowing recipes clipped from now-defunct magazines are dragged from the backs of kitchen drawers. That experiment you always wanted to try with pork rinds and a banana can now be tested on some poor unsuspecting fool. You can't wait to see the look on their faces when you tell them that the secret ingredient in your dessert topping is a thin slice of raw onion. You also dreamt of providing a fifty-foot long buffet with NO DISH REPEATED along its length. Fair enough, but there are some party dishes that no one on this planet (with the exception of traffic wardens) should be forced to endure. We are here but for a brief time. Why spoil it with something on a paper plate from the depths of Cocktail Stick Hell?

These, then, are the dishes to avoid at any party.

Learn to recognise them at fifty paces in dim lighting.

Never place one on a paper plate as it will eat right through, just like that gooey stuff which corroded through the floor of the spaceship in 'ALIEN'.

IT CAME FROM THE POTATO SALAD

~ ~ ~

MMMMMM, yum, it looks like a harmless melange of

42

... *something on a paper plate*
from Cocktail Stick Hell.

43

cut-up potato in sour cream and mayo. But BE WARNED! Somewhere in there lurk tasty little surprises with which the host experimentally embellished the original recipe. They're cunningly disguised within the creamy gunk just waiting for you to bite into them. We're talking ROLLMOPS! UNSOAKED PIECES OF DRIED APRICOT! ANCHOVIES! UNCRUSHED PIECES OF GARLIC CLOVE! MALTESERS! I think I'm going to be sick.

THE SNACK FROM ANOTHER WORLD
~ ~ ~

A square of rubbery Dutch cheese, on top of a sugary chunk of canned pineapple, skewered with a cocktail stick, stuck with dozens of others into a grapefruit covered with silver foil. You don't eat the grapefruit, or the cocktail stick. But you might consider it as an alternative.

THE PICKLES THAT TIME FORGOT
~ ~ ~

Onions, little sweet white ones in a jar. Red cabbage. Banana chutney with peppers in. Anything that has been soaked in vinegar for months. OK, you may expect to find them at a party given by defecting Russians, but anyone else who serves them thinking that we actually enjoy chasing something around a paper plate for ten minutes with a fork before it jumps down the front of our shirt has to be one above plant life.

DEVIL SARDINES FROM MARS
~ ~ ~

Avoid any party where there is a sardine buffet dish. Avoid contact with anyone who has been to a party where sardines have been served.

Detour around any street where you suspect a sardine-oriented party may be in progress.

Treat people who have been known to serve a sardine dish at their party with the sneering contempt you normally reserve for dealing with the telephone company. People who serve sardines at parties should be doomed to a lifetime of motorway food, curried pub lunches, spots and guilt-riddled poorly timed sex.

Well, that's my opinion anyway.

THE CRACKER THAT CHALLENGED THE WORLD
~   ~   ~

The flat surface of a cracker encourages people of unsound culinary ideas to pile on combinations of such conflicting texture and taste that the only way to avoid shooting the first mouthful across the room and sticking it to the opposite wall is to test an initial cracker somewhere private. In the toilet, perhaps. Know these deadly combos:

Anything fishy that is not caviar i.e. fishpaste . . . or . . . SARDINE!

Sausage slice and onion ring.

A folded-over piece of processed cheese and a gherkin.

Anything savoury with peanut butter.

Blue cheese and spam.

I once filled my plate from a very gaudy buffet in a spectacularly vulgar, expensive and nasty Miami hotel (the name of which I shall be happy to post to anyone planning to visit that area) only to find that the creamed vegetables I had loaded on to my plate with the beef weren't vegetables at all but sweet desserts. The regular eaters around me

45

wanted to know how I could possibly mix horseradish with candied mango, beef slices and blueberry trifle. It tasted the way warm plasticene smells.

I don't know how you feel after reading that, but I feel really poorly.

THE CHEAPSKATE'S PARTY BUFFET
~ ~ ~

These are the dishes which let you know that your host/ess is a cheap bum.

1. <u>Pseudo Prawn Dip</u>
Made by mixing bottle of ketchup with bottle of salad cream and pouring into dip bowl.

2. <u>Crisps in Shallow Trays</u>
Apart from the fact that serving crisps is a bit naff to begin with, putting them into trays normally reserved for dried rose petals is unforgivably cheap.

3. <u>Rice, Peas and Raisins</u>
The Cheap Host/ess is apparently under the belief that this constitutes a party dish by itself, and that guests will eat it by the hundredweight. It is your duty to prove that they are mistaken. I suggest bringing some of your own along and actually *adding* to the dish. They'll be eating it for weeks.

4. <u>Gouda and Edam</u>
Trust the Cheap Host/ess to buy cheese in foundation stone sized blocks which taste like the rubber you find inside golf balls.

46

5. Day-Old French Bread

Day-old French bread is cheaper. It is not for eating. It is for scouring paintwork.

6. Luncheon Meat

Oh, all right, just a small slice. Thanks. No, that's plenty. Mmmm. Do you have a cat?

The truly Cheap Host/ess will also lay out tiny crackers in the shape of fish, about a hundred thousand Twiglets, and wine in cardboard boxes bought on last summer's cycling tour of France.

7. Sour grapes

PARTY DRINKS
~ ~ ~

The general rule of thumb about taking drinks to parties is:

1. If you're an impoverished art student, you take a bottle of cheap cider with you and spend the evening drinking someone else's special strength beer.

2. If you're between college and employment you take a bottle of dry white wine, unless you can find an ancient bottle of hand-warm Arabian burgundy down the back of the airing cupboard which you can palm off.

3. If you're working, you take a huge party can of bitter and drink it all by yourself, guarding the can between sips by sitting on it.

Party Law dictates that there will always be either far too much or far too little for guests to drink. You either have to throw another party the following week to clear the refrigerator of bottles, or halfway through the evening you find guests staring dejectedly into paper cups filled with crême de menthe.

COCKTAILS
~ ~ ~

Now that cocktails have once more become fashionable, you'll find that the best way to drink them is in the home rather than having them served by a sour-faced, out-of-work actor in a trendified pub called something like 'Knockers' or 'Floozies' that's been decorated like a 1930's public lavatory and then covered in airbrushed prints of Californian palm trees. Each drink here costs roughly as much as a pair of decent running shoes.

The owners of these overpriced emporia sit around trying to come up with the most stupid and embarrassing names they can think of to call their cocktails, just so that they can have a good laugh listening to you ordering them. And unless you're a cocktail expert, you don't know that a Flying Tonguecrusher is Brandy, Lemon juice and Cherry Heering garnished with a radish, do you? They could pour it into a half of Guinness and you wouldn't be any the wiser. Stick to shaking them up at parties.

THE WORST COCKTAIL EVER INVENTED
~ ~ ~

Stuart invented a cocktail that is lime green and tastes of battered fish. If you add Kahlua to it, it turns the same colour and consistency as the slime you find in the bottom of a vase of sunflowers after they have been standing for over a week. I think that it had dark rum, Midori, gin, lime syrup and falernum in it as well as the contents of a small blue bottle from Spain which had a crystalline branch inside and smelled of pine disinfectant.

Another great cocktail is the Alabama Slammer, a popular American nightclub drink which you toss down the throat in a shot glass. It is made with white rum, vodka and cranberry juice, is bright pink and tastes like liquid paraffin mixed with fruit juice. You might try stirring it with a firelighter to give it extra body. A few of these and you can wave goodbye to the weekend, even if it's only Wednesday.

... invented a cocktail that's lime
green and tastes of battered fish.

50

I can recommend the following recipe as the perfect Revolting Cocktail:

MINT OPALESCENT
~ ~ ~

12 PARTS GIN
 4 PARTS LEMON JUICE
 2 PARTS GRENADINE
 2 EGG WHITES
 1 TSP MINT EXTRACT
    (Or two 'Wintergreen Mixture' boiled sweets)

Add the gin, lemon juice and grenadine to the egg white, add plenty of crushed ice and shake vigorously. Strain into a tall cocktail glass over mint or boiled sweets.

The end result is a strangely sinister looking drink, perfect for cleaning up old jewellery, dipping arrow heads into, and serving to hated elderly relatives.

RULES OF SERVING PARTY DRINKS
~ ~ ~

1. If you borrow wineglasses from the local pub, there will always be five glasses missing when you return them.

2. If you point to a full bottle of Scotch and tell the guests to help themselves, it will last exactly nine minutes to the second.

3. When you open a large can of beer, it will spray over the person you most seek to impress.

4. Never stir a cocktail with your finger before handing it over.

5. Know that it is possible to pour a beer without leaving a six inch head floating above an inch of booze.

6. Never try to cross a dance-floor carrying four

drinks, particularly if guests are doing the can-can.

There's another Revolting Cocktail called a Mississippi River Bottom, involving iced tea, rum and something vaguely medicinal like Kaolin, but time has mercifully blotted it from my memory. Pass me a beer, would you?

8. Impossible tiny street maps that get read beneath lamp posts

OK, this won't take long. You are sitting in the car squinting at a hopelessly inadequate, poorly reproduced Xerox of the street area in which the party is supposed to be taking place. You are well over an hour late. It is raining. According to the badly drawn diagram at the bottom of the invitation, you are presently parked in a street which does not exist. You have been round the block four times. Each time, you have failed to find the road in which this mythical dwelling filled with people having fun stands. Indeed, you are beginning to think that the whole invitation is a cheap practical joke. Well, I shall tell you where you are going wrong.

Remember this solution to the problem, for it may be used every single time such a situation occurs.

WHY YOU CAN'T FIND THE PARTY

~ ~ ~

1. You went round the crescent and it came to a dead end, right? That's because the house isn't in the crescent at all. The road you are looking for extends across the High Street, but the person who drew the map forgot to put in the High Street, so just go to the end of the road, cross the street which isn't marked and the house is there on the left.

According to the diagram, you are presently
parked in a street which does not exist.

2. The road is marked in the A – Z but it's so short that the lettering is all squashed up and you can't read it.

3. Before you came to the road where the party is, you turned left. WRONG! It's half left. It's also One Way, from the other end, and has no street lamps.

4. It's the upstairs flat with the unmarked bell, and the reason you can't hear any party noise coming from upstairs is because their lounge is at the back of the house.

5. The party is being held in a corner house. The entrance you want is in a side-street, unmarked on your map.

Still, it's better that you have written instructions for locating the party than taking directions over the telephone from a scatty friend. To whit, directions received from my friend Sally who lives in Broadstairs:

> *It's simple. Go left at the roundabout to Margate, and when you get to the seafront, turn – left or right, I forget which, still you can't go straight on, ha ha, past Butlins, left at the T-junction by a cabbage field, only it's night so you won't be able to see the cabbages, but there's a scarecrow which you can see, only somebody stole it, then you have to turn right. You've got Northdown Park on your left now, my left not your left of course, and keep your eyes open for a pub. I can't remember it's name but they're famous for their seafood, then you come to a fork in the road and you take a left turning. I forgot to say that there was another T-junction where you had to turn right, which eventually brings you out by that other pub, the name of which escapes me, but I know you've been there. I forgot to say that earlier on there was a lighthouse. Oh, and when you see that, it's another left.*

And you're suddenly in our road, and we're the ones with the night scented stock in the front garden.

I headed for that house armed with an Ordnance Survey map, a Good Pub Guide and a volume on Britain's hedgerows, and I *still* never found the place.

9. Party themes

Original and unusual fancy dress parties are a great way of getting a roomful of total strangers to loosen up and have fun. It's very hard to keep the conversation strictly to our involvement in supplying arms for the latest South African border dispute when the person you're talking to is dressed as a bunny.

Here follow a few ideas for fancy dress parties with special themes.

1. A NIGHT IN THE TROPICS
~ ~ ~

Up with the central heating, palm fronds everywhere, Kid Creole on the stereo, mosquito netting over the buffet, tropical kit for the commander and his wife, sola topis and sunsets, puttees and punkahs, and don't try to serve a pint of beer in a pineapple. They roll over.

2. NOEL COWARD PARTY
~ ~ ~

It's everyone into evening wear, thirties style, and let's all be brittle. The best way to become a Bright Young Thing is to lean on the piano with a brandy (if male) and interminably arrange a bowl of hyacinths (if female). Then everyone gets snappish and insulting, we all call each other cads, prigs and bounders, and then we all drag each other off into the garden in twos while a tall elegant woman collapses on the ottoman with a cry of, 'I simply can't stand it! I'm going to *die!*' Good music for such a party; Ivor Novello, or Jessie Mathews singing 'Gangway!'

3. THE LIFEBOAT PARTY

~ ~ ~

Dress exactly as you were when the Titanic foundered. Slightly tattered evening wear is good, slightly askew formal attire with perhaps one crucial item missing is better. Choose anything from that 'dressed-in-a-hurry' look to the 'Stuck-in-a-lifeboat-with-a-packet-of-sea-biscuits-and-Gloria-Swanson' desperation.

4. WWII PARTY

~ ~ ~

I say, let's all come as RAF pilots and WRENS. Spiffy can tunnel out of the kitchen using a spoon, Pongo and I will build a wooden horse in the lounge, and Fatty can distract the Krauts by dive-bombing the guests with sausage rolls. No talking after lights out!

5. 'B' MOVIE STAR PARTY

~ ~ ~

Uh oh, can't come as Gable or Monroe here. You are, however, allowed to attend as Evelyn Ankers, John Agar or Rondo Hatton. Obscure, forgettable forties and fifties musicals and science fiction film scores to be played all night. Try coming as the giant lobster from 'TEENAGERS FROM OUTER SPACE'.

6. MICROCHIP PARTY

~ ~ ~

It's tiny, it's Japanese and it feels like it's happening ten years too early. Why, it's the *future*! Electronic music, space age leisure wear and a hideous quartz crystal watch are a start, but spending the evening in a Sony Walkman could be considered a tad unsociable.

7. CIRCUS CIRCUS
~ ~ ~

Sawdust on the floor, bunting from the ceiling and try holding a conversation through a loudhailer. Roll up, roll up, see the incredible Fat Lady, the amazing Dog-Faced Boy, the drunken Tumblers and who is that on the flying trapeze? Tell your bank manager to get down off the mantelpiece.

8. OUT-OF-DATE PARTY
~ ~ ~

Feeling jaded? Life passing you by? Unable to keep up with the modern pace? Tough shit, Life doesn't care whether you keep up or not, so why bother? Throw an Out-of-Date party, where everyone wears the worst, most dated clothes they can find. Platform shoes, blue eye shadow, hula hoops, flared trousers, spats, legwarmers, clogs and white PVC mini-skirts. Boy, the Fashion Gods will be angry tonight!

Themes to be avoided

1. TARTS AND VICARS
~ ~ ~

Along with anything else where men expect women to dress up as schoolgirls in order to work through their stumped, gnarled adolescent fantasies.

2. GENDER-SWITCH PARTIES
~ ~ ~

Women don't enjoy them at all and men enjoy them far too much.

Women don't enjoy them at all
and men enjoy them far too much.

60

3. BAD TASTE PARTIES
~ ~ ~

It is no longer shocking to attend a party dressed as a much loved, recently murdered famous figure. The whole of our lifestyle passed over into bad taste several years ago, and this fact has rendered all such parties invalid.

4. BEATLES SONGS PARTIES
~ ~ ~

Hey man, let's all come as Beatles song titles.
Who are you, man?
Well, I'm wearing like, yellow loons, and scuba goggles.
    I'm Yellow Submarine, man.
Oh, Wow!

Also to be steered well clear of are the sort of occasions which get featured in the *Tatler*, those parties populated entirely by giggling fat young men called the Hon. Something, and those extraordinarily plain daughters of the rich, all named after flowers and wearing the latest grotesque designer fad.

PARTY GAMES
~ ~ ~

Uh oh, it's organised fun. It's best to stick to Charades, or anything with teams, just as long as the teams are not males against females, because that gets too much like Real Fighting At Home.

When you team up for Charades, you will find that you have one person on your side who cannot act things out properly. This is the person who forgot that *Gone With The Wind* was a book and a film, the person who told the other side there were five syllables in *Pygmalion*. Not to

61

worry though, the other team has someone like this as well. Charades should be played until the first accusation of cheating, whereupon someone will offer to make coffee, thus ending the game.

Card games are great fun if you are over 90 or have lost 75 per cent of your motor movement. Any game which involves a lot of counting, fake money, pencils and paper, more than five rules, and markers shaped like racing cars is too complicated for a party. Hunt The Slipper and Sardines should be left to the under fives. There are much more realistic games you can play:

1. PIN THE BLAME ON THE PARTNER

This is a terrific party game in which you have to guess which person in the room your partner would most consider committing carnal rudeness with behind your back. There are no rules to the game beyond the mandatory muttering of the sentence, 'You couldn't take your eyes off him/her all night', and it can be played all the way home, and again at breakfast the next morning. Dirty fighting is allowed.

2. EARLY GUEST'S KNOCK

This game begins when someone shouts, 'Oh my God, look at the time, they'll be here any minute!' Any number of people may join in this marathon, which involves getting in each other's way in the kitchen, moving the sofa out of the lounge without ripping the lintels from the doors, removing the good glasses and smashing two in the process, and hiding the Chivas Regal where at least three people will find it. The game is won by the person who remembers to put an ashtray in the toilet.

3. NAME DROPPER'S DELIGHT
~ ~ ~

How many famous people can you weave into the fabric of your opening conversation with other party guests? Bonus points are awarded for intimating that you are on first name terms with the famous. First prize goes to anyone who can get the name 'Dickie Attenborough' into a sentence before anyone else.

4. OUTSTAYED WELCOMES
~ ~ ~

Look! It's nearly dawn! The host has gone to bed. The hostess sporadically falls sideways in a fit of tiredness. As the room lightens you ask if there's more coffee in the pot and continue to lay out your argument in favour of unilateral disarmament, even though nobody is listening. The arm of the record player lowers itself and begins to play Carole King's 'Tapestry' for the seventeenth time in succession. The winner is the person who comes out with a plausible excuse for having stayed so long, like, 'We would have left ages ago, but your husband was screwing someone on our coats.'

5. CRASHDANCE!
~ ~ ~

Who can come up with the silliest and most dangerous new dance routine?

Apparently everyone, by the look of it. No prizes for dated Mick Jagger impersonations. Or Rod Stewart Struts. An honourable mention, though, to the girl who flashdanced herself down the hall and out of the upstairs window. Likewise the woman who came dressed as Olivia Neutered-Tom. The one who snagged a legwarmer on the buffet table and dragged three people down with her when she fell over.

The first prize goes to the guy with the bizarre arm movements who acts like he's operating hand puppets and manages to punch a tray of drinks out of the host's hands in a moment of dance-crazed enthusiasm.

At stag parties, men like to play games which involve drinking enormous quantities of alcohol as fast as they can until they pass out. They hire strippers, then laugh to cover their embarrassment when the show gets raunchy. They swear a lot, act like children and smell weird by the end of the evening.

At hen nights, the group quickly divides into women who want to talk about men and make-up, and women who don't. The women who do don't understand why the women who don't don't. They all get drunk too, and towards the end of the evening they start screaming with laughter, and although they don't swear as much, they come up with much *much* ruder conversational topics than men.

10. The top ten party guests of all time

If you could have anyone in history attend your party, who would you choose?

1. JESUS CHRIST
~ ~ ~
Will lend dignity and reverence to the proceedings. Also useful when the wine gets low.

2. SIR JOHN GIELGUD
~ ~ ~
Legendary theatrical figure, masses of fascinating reminiscences, much to discuss, has he seen the full version of 'Caligula', etc.

3. MARCEL MARCEAU
~ ~ ~
Won't interrupt your stories.

4. STEVEN SPIELBERG
~ ~ ~
He's just *dying* to hear your idea for a screenplay.

5. BOB MARLEY
~ ~ ~
Can organise the music and, er, have you got a cigarette on you, Bob?

6. MARILYN MONROE
~ ~ ~
You can discuss her views on feminism, world politics, the Kennedy connection, the CIA and really tight angora sweaters.

. . . won't interrupt your stories.

66

7. KARL MARX
~ ~ ~
Oh, wait a minute, not him, the one who was in Horse Feathers.

8. ELIZABETH TAYLOR
~ ~ ~
So that you won't be stuck with any leftover buffet quiches and pâtés the next day.

9. FRED ASTAIRE
~ ~ ~
That should put paid to any upstaging on the dance-floor!

10. IDI AMIN
~ ~ ~
With him on the door as a bouncer threatening to cut gatecrashers' heads off you shouldn't have any trouble.

11. 'Surprise!'

THE HORRIBLE TRUTH ABOUT SURPRISE PARTIES

~ ~ ~

They don't work.

The reason for this is simple. Not many people actually *like* surprises.

A friend of mine recently planned to celebrate his thirtieth birthday by going home for the evening and staying in with a bottle of champagne. Upon returning to his house from work, he slipped into the bedroom, removed his clothes, put on his favourite raggedy-ol'-underwear-for-schlepping-around-the-house-in, and upon entering his bathroom for the purpose of sundry ablutions, was greeted by the sight of twenty-six people, including his parents, standing in the bath with Polaroid cameras, screaming. He was not amused.

If you are thinking of planning a surprise party for a friend, bear in mind that the following schedule is typical of the events surrounding a surprise party.

It is Roger's birthday. David, a friend, has telephoned all Roger's acquaintances and has asked them to attend a surprise party to be held at Roger's house. He tells them to arrive no later than seven o'clock. Now read on . . .

... was greeted by the sight of twenty-six
people standing in the bath.

69

THE SURPRISE PARTY TIME SCHEDULE

~ ~ ~

TIME	WHAT'S HAPPENING TO ROGER . . .	. . . AND WHAT'S HAPPENING BACK AT HIS HOUSE
6.00 PM	Roger finishes work and wanders around the office dejectedly looking for someone to go for a drink with on this, his birthday. As his colleagues are all rushing home to change for his party, he meets with no luck. But this has been taken into account by his friends, as . . .	The kitchen is a frenzy of activity. The wraps have come off of the canapes in transit and no one can find any foil to keep them fresh. It also transpires that nobody thought of napkins.
6.15 PM	Old friend Maggie appears and offers to take Roger out for a drink. Roger moans about his friends all having excuses for not being with him tonight. He is skilfully manoeuvred into a bar by Maggie.	Roger's sister cuts the top off her thumb trying to open a tin of sardines and is taken to hospital for stitches.
6.30 PM	Maggie warns Roger that he is drinking too quickly on an empty stomach. Roger orders drinks for all the bar staff.	While looking for a teatowel in the spare room, Roger's girlfriend finds a pile of torrid letters addressed to Roger from another woman and threatens to go home until the others manage to talk her out of it.
6.45 PM	Maggie and Roger are knocking back doubles at the bar, with Maggie protesting heavily but unable to alleviate Roger's deepening depression.	Panic as someone realises that they put the food into the oven at six but failed to turn the gas on. They manage to squeeze it all on to the top shelf and put the gas on 'HIGH'.
7.00 PM	Maggie telephones the house to make sure that all the preparations are going smoothly. While she is out of the bar, the bar staff buy Roger a triple brandy to cheer him up on his birthday.	Nearly all the guests have assembled, and the party organiser, in whom the occasion has brought out an innate officiousness, refuses to let anyone have a drink, let alone touch the food.
7.15 PM	Roger orders drinks with umbrellas in and toasts absent friends alphabetically in a loud and tasteless manner while Maggie tries to get him to leave.	A non heat-proof casserole dish explodes on the cooker. Eleven people are showered with boiling chilli con carne.
7.30 PM	Roger is lining little umbrellas along the bar and recalling previous unpleasant situations where his friends have let him down. Maggie calls the house again and asks if everyone has arrived, because Roger is getting drunk.	Yes, comes the reply. Everyone is here except June and Michael, and they're always late for everything.

TIME	WHAT'S HAPPENING TO ROGER . . .	. . . AND WHAT'S HAPPENING BACK AT HIS HOUSE
7.30 PM	Well, says Maggie, they had better not turn up any later than eight. Did the DJ have any trouble setting up the portable disco?	Disco? Comes the reply. What disco?
7.45 PM	Before she can stop him, Roger orders Pina Coladas for the entire bar and falls off his stool.	Organiser relents and allows the guests to have a drink before they lynch him. This starts a free-for-all on the food which he dares not try to stop.
7.55 PM	Maggie is sitting in the Men's Toilet pouring cold water on Roger and slapping him around the face.	Guests are panicked by the sight of the DJ dragging disco equipment through the doors of the building mere moments before the guest of honour is due to arrive.
8.05 PM	Roger insists that he now feels fine. He rises before the mirror, combs his hair, straightens his tie and promptly throws up in an unusual and spectacular manner.	The DJ, panicked by the sight of guests hanging out of the upstairs window screaming at him to hurry up, puts a door handle through his left woofer and threatens to charge them for it.
8.15 PM	Roger announced that being ill did him the world of good, although his words are given scant credence by his complexion, which is currently that shade of luminous white you normally only find on television screens after the night's programmes have ended.	Everyone is hushed and hiding in the kitchen cupboard, except for one really fat girl who said she'd be more comfortable under the kitchen table.
8.35 PM	Maggie and Roger are in a taxi. Roger has passed out and Maggie can't remember the address but insists that she'll recognise the house when she sees it.	False alarm. Everyone screams and jumps out on the late arrivals, Michael and June. Then they all get back into the cupboard. Non-appearance of fat girl suggests that her crouched position under the table has either given her cramp or caused her to drop off to sleep.
8.50 PM	Maggie thinks she recognises the house, but feels that perhaps it is not the right street.	Someone has to get out of the cupboard to stop fat girl under the table from snoring.
9.00 PM	Maggie finally locates Roger's house and drags him from the cab with great difficulty while cab driver sits and watches.	Fearing that their air supply is running out, someone in the cupboard suggests that they give it five more minutes, then go home. Everyone else agrees.

TIME	WHAT'S HAPPENING TO ROGER...	...AND WHAT'S HAPPENING BACK AT HIS HOUSE
9.05 PM	Roger comes back to life after falling over and landing on his keys.	A unanimous vote decides that the guests leave their cupboard prison and help themselves to the booze.
9.07 PM	Roger and Maggie are heard on the stairs.	There is a concerted rush back into the cupboard amidst much shushing.
9.08 PM	Roger comes into his apartment	Guests are unable to get the cupboard door open.
9.08½ PM	Roger pulls down his trousers prior to heading for the bathroom and passes out on the floor.	Cupboard door is successfully unwedged and guests jump out to sing Happy Birthday to a startled Maggie.

THE AFTERMATH
~ ~ ~

The party continues as the semi-asphyxiated guests gorge themselves and dance around the inert body of the birthday boy, who next day will have no recollection of having seen any of his old friends, but who will wonder forever after what a top-shelf full of forgotten, burned black quiches were doing in his oven.

His friends, embarrassed about the whole affair, will deny ever having seen him that night.

And . . . Maggie will get left with the clearing up.

12. Altered states

DR*G TAKING AT PARTIES

~ ~ ~

Some people – not the author, you understand – but SOME people, aware that sudden exposure to a roomful of complete strangers can cause spectacular changes in one's mental state, seek to cushion the experience through recourse to the miracle of modern chemistry.

The variety of stimulants and suppressants that can be introduced into the human body is extraordinary, as can be the range of positive and adverse effects they can have on one's organs.

Modern chemicals allow you to fix the mood of the evening – from pleasure and peacefulness, through exhilaration to depression and dog-tiredness. Naturally, the author does not advocate the use of these recreational 'enjoyment enhancers', although today you'll find the most likely people to be offering you dr*gs are your parents, catching up on the forbidden pleasures of the past. You should see our place at Christmas. But enough of this idle banter. You should know what you're getting into here. There is one golden rule with dr*gs; FOR EVERY ACTION THERE IS A REACTION. In other words, you can't race the engine without wearing down the parts. Bearing that in mind, cast your eye over the following simple guide:

WHAT'S UP YOUR NOSE, DOC
~ ~ ~
Or, A Simple Guide to the Effects of Party Dr*gs

1. SYMPTOMS: You feel pleasantly euphoric. The people around you seem nice and friendly. You, in turn, are charming, and not without the odd amusing anecdote with which to speed the conversation along. It's nice and warm, and you're enjoying yourself.

CAUSE: You've had a couple of drinks . . . and actually, you were in a pretty good mood to begin with.

2. SYMPTOMS: Boy, you're really on form tonight. Funny, caustic even, and cute. And sexy. Yet there are people here who seem immune to your charms. After a few minutes with you, they excuse themselves and leave your company.

CAUSE: You have had a lot to drink. Quit while you're ahead. Go home. Do not pass GO or the drinks cabinet.

3. SYMPTOMS: You must sit down, you feel so tired. If you move your head quickly, everything blurs. You feel lightheaded, as if you were on top of a mountain . . . but you're only eighteen feet and two flights of stairs above sea level.

CAUSE: You are drunk. You pig. Get a friend to take you to the bathroom and run your head under the cold tap. Be nice to them otherwise they may leave your head in the basin. And stop feeling sorry for yourself. We've all done it before. Even your mother. *Especially* your mother.

4. SYMPTOMS: Somebody stuck this small brown bottle up your nose while you were dancing, and suddenly

74

you feel totally wild. The music, however bad, suddenly becomes your favourite track of all time, and you dance like a deranged aerobics instructor. The only trouble is, you have a vague feeling that if you could see inside your chest, your heart would appear to be pumping as if it were an old piece of liver with electrodes stuck in it.

CAUSE: The tell-tale smell on the dance-floor reveals the presence of bottles of Poppers, ex-wonder thrill (and of the cheapest kind) of the seventies, and now somewhat in disrepute, owing to the knowledge that it merely speeds up the heart for a few moments and causes the blood to rush Niagara-like around the body. Besides which, it can cause splitting headaches, and is immensely offensive to non-users due to its all-pervading 'Gymnasium-changing-room-on-a-hot-afternoon' aroma. Available over the counter, though hilariously sold as a 'room purifier'.

5. SYMPTOMS: You are completely numb. Earlier you walked into a wall and didn't feel a thing. You think you may have left your backbone in your other jacket. You feel like you've been filleted, but do fish get this sleepy? Look, there's a dent in the fireguard where you just tripped, and HEY! A nosebleed! Where did that come from? Oh, it's OK, it's from the floor which just came up to say hello.

CAUSE: What we are dealing with here is a first-time experience with a Quaalude. It was a little white tablet – you remember – someone broke it in half and shared it with you. So-called because they were designed to give you a QUiet interLUDE, these have only just been taken off the US market as a legal drug. Don't worry, just find a nice big comfortable sofa and fall asleep. Try not to bump

... *walked into a wall earlier and
didn't feel a thing.*

into too many things getting there unless you want to wake up with leopardskin legs.

6. SYMPTOMS: You feel, like, totally mellow and, like really in control of your personal space, man, because you're having, like, this totally awesome and tubular experience with these people around you who are, like, really attuned to the vibes you're giving out – and what is rilly, rilly so boss is that this totally vicious chick is coming on to you (or if you're a chick, this totally foxy dude). You feel at one with the universe, man. Except that you have a tendency to fall down.

CAUSE: You have been smoking very strong grass, and have deluded yourself under its influence into thinking that you are Californian. If you have to feel Californian, you should feel very Santa Monica and Robertson, very Melrose and Spaulding. You should *never* feel very Ventura or very Burton Way. But remember, pseudo-American accents sound terrible on someone from Birmingham.

7. SYMPTOMS: Everything is wonderful here! The people are wonderful, the music is wonderful, and you, why YOU are wonderful! You have so much to say, and you want to say it all at once. You can't talk fast enough. It's very interesting just standing here being alive. Except that you seem to have this cold. You must do because your nose is running.

CAUSE: Well, it looks like cocaine just enhanced your evening.

<u>A few DON'Ts:</u>

DON'T get the straw stuck up your nose.

DON'T ask the gathering if anyone has a razor blade.

DON'T cut it on a formica topped kitchen counter.

DON'T come out of the bathroom making flamboyant nasal hawking noises.

DON'T share it.

DON'T sneeze on the mirror.

DON'T snort it through a rolled banknote (the placing of currency in the nostrils is considered by some to be vulgar).

DON'T cut it with Ajax to make it go further.

As for other party 'liveners', hallucinogens are great if you've been invited to a party for goblins and unicorns, and speedy things are fine if you hate the idea of having to sleep nights over the coming week.

Think of party dr*gs as a video game where the chosen dr*g is the destroyer ship, and the meteors being blasted are your brain cells. The score is up to you.

THE MUNCHIES
~ ~ ~

The inevitable penalty for so much energy burning is the overwhelming desire to have oral intercourse with a half-pound cheeseburger at three o'clock in the morning. Naturally, you will be unable to obtain such a tasty snack, and when you return home will find yourself confronted with the contents of your kitchen cabinet – namely, a packet of stale crispbread and some very old pickles in cloudy vinegar . . . WHICH YOU WILL PROCEED TO EAT!

I used to live near a 24-hour supermarket, where, at Disco Witching Hour, clusters of stoned freaks could be spotted at the dairy chiller attempting to rip the heat-sealed plastic from packets of Jack Cheese with their teeth in order to get a calory fix before reaching the checkout counter. Not a pretty sight, but a fascinating one, like watching vultures feeding.

13. The office Christmas party

Assuming you're employed, there's a good chance that you'll be invited to attend the office Christmas party, and against your better judgement you'll probably end up going. What on earth for?

You must have a reason for doing this, and it can't be because you want to meet new people, so why are you risking such a dangerous assignation? If it's for one of the following reasons, you must beware of the consequences.

	REASON FOR ATTENDING	CONSEQUENCE OF ATTENDING
1.	You have been sexually attracted to someone in your office for months, and plan to make your move under cover of drunkenness (either yours or theirs).	That person will reject your offer so violently that for months after you'll be forced to hide in the photostat room every time you see him or her coming towards you in the corridor.
2.	You wish to show your fellow employees that there's another, more fun side to the boring worker they see every day in the office.	Your total change of character at the party will lead your workmates to think that you have some kind of weird split personality, and they will stay well away from you, especially when you're sharpening pencils.
3.	You plan to corner your boss and show your conscientiousness over your work with a view to promotion or a rise.	Your boss will mistake your interest in his conversation for sexual attraction, and this will lead to all kinds of new office dangers in the weeks ahead, i.e. being goosed at the coffee machine.
4.	You have nothing better to do.	You will leave the party with one of the mailboys and he'll tell everyone what you're like in bed. After this, every time you take a letter down to be mailed, you'll hear laughter as you leave the room.

At the Christmas party, just as in daily office life, there will be a strict office hierarchy in force. This is where true office sexism comes in. You may accept an invitation to join the bosses for a drink, but you may not extend the same offer downwards. In this way, it is acceptable for a senior male executive to dance with the pretty new office typist, but not for a female executive to get frigging with a junior mailboy. And of course, there are certain things you must never, ever do at office parties . . .

THINGS YOU MUST NEVER DO AT THE OFFICE CHRISTMAS PARTY
~ ~ ~

1. Have sex in one of the upstairs offices, then fall asleep on top of your partner until work starts the next morning.

2. Stage a show in which you sing a savagely satirical song about your boss's weight problem.

3. Get drunk and tell people what you've really thought of them all year.

4. Call for so much champagne that you appear much more affluent than your income allows, thereby causing everyone to think that you're freelancing on the side.

5. Tell anyone a really personal secret which you would never have dreamt of mentioning had you been sober.

The Christmas office party is a great time to gather blackmail material, because it's the time when people inadvertently reveal that they've been having inter-office affairs. Watch for crying secretaries and nervous filing clerks, studiously casual introductions between bosses and typists who are trying to look as if they haven't been going to dark Italian restaurants with each other for months.

81

... drunkenly revealed a very personal
secret to a work colleague.

Take notes. You can tell much about your fellow workers from the degree of caution that they decide to throw to the winds at the office party:

ABANDONMENT OF CAUTION AT OFFICE CHRISTMAS PARTIES: LEVEL CHART
≈   ≈   ≈

	MAILBOY	SECRETARY	MANAGER	CHAIRMAN	RESULT
LEVEL 1	Waves mistletoe at every woman in the room.	Cautiously dances around her handbag.	Corners boss for ages.	Dances in modern style, i.e. Twist, Mashed Potato.	Healthy display of Christmas zeal is regarded as OK.
LEVEL 2	Invites punk girlfriend along.	Takes off shoes. Laughs hysterically at anything.	Corners boss interminably. Starts making suggestions about how to run the place.	Attempts slow dance with receptionist and cops a feel.	Still basically OK, although a watchful eye is now being kept by seniors.
LEVEL 3	Spends evening with tongue down her throat.	Leads Conga line, screaming a lot.	Seen heading for Xerox room with typist.	Attempts to breakdance.	Very cool reception at work the next day.
LEVEL 4	Openly takes drugs, drops trousers at bosses.	Dress straps fall down, molested on dance floor.	Seen heading for Xerox room with mailboy.	Suffers massive coronary.	Major drama next day.
LEVEL 5	Noisily throws up. Knocks over beer can pyramid as he passes out.	Hysterical crying, has to be slapped.	Appearance of wife and humiliating punch-up in public.	D.O.A.	Termination of employment.

14. Fighting at parties

'DON'T MAKE A SCENE!'

~ ~ ~

Given the number of diverse personalities cooped up in a room together, the number of throats and brains drenched in alcohol, the heat and the noise of the average party, is it any surprise that cross words are exchanged, often by the most rational and outwardly normal characters present?

You must learn to recognise the darkening clouds of discord and seed them with the soothing voice of rationality. *Tell* him that these days it is no longer fashionable to hit a woman. *Tell* her that you've heard she swings a mean right hook and would love to see it in action.

Women are much better at fighting in public than men, being sharper, faster and more original in their approach. A man will only argue for so long before reverting to a neanderthal state and lashing out, whereas a woman will happily resort to the casual tossing of a cocktail into the lap, or even – and I remember a genuine instance of this – running out of the house with the man's car keys and flinging them down the nearest drain. Real fighting at parties requires spirit, and above all a total lack of embarrassment about airing one's most intimate affairs in public. Party fighting gives the guests something to talk about and remember for months, and for true theatricality should include screamed revelations of the kind that can shatter a twenty-year marriage.

... *total lack of embarrassment about airing*
their most intimate affairs in public.

Real party fighters also know when to stop. A woman I know calmly sat and drank while her husband heaped abuse on her at a dinner party, knowing that the particular occasion in question did not call for undignified behaviour on her part. She did, however, succeed in running him over in the car park afterwards.

Your natural intuition will help you to pick out those guests who have the ability to scream about their sex lives at the tops of their voices at cocktail parties without feeling the slightest bit self-conscious. This handy guide will supplement that intuition.

TROUBLE SPOTTING AT PARTIES
~ ~ ~

1. A divorced guest gives you the rundown on his/her sex life between the time you open the front door and when the two of you reach the end of the hall.

DANGER!

This person is desperate, and will take the first refusal of a sexual liaison from a guest so venomously to heart that everyone in the room will get to hear about it.

FORECAST:

A screaming fit, face slapping, a lot of tears in the toilet.

2. A couple across the room are talking to each other in tense rasping voices through clenched teeth. She walks away from time to time and he pulls her back by grabbing her arm.

DANGER!

She is about to accuse him of adultery, something she has been wanting to do for nearly two years now.

FORECAST:

I see a drink in the face, the words 'Bitch' and 'Bastard' used as proper nouns, and four people to hold them apart.

3. A drunken man is trying to monopolise the attention of a woman who is obviously with her boyfriend, who glares on silently.

DANGER!

The boyfriend's temper is legendary, the drunk is slow to catch on, and you had better remove all sharp objects from the room double quick.

FORECAST:

Two loose teeth and a wired jaw are winging their way towards the oblivious drunk, who would be more seriously injured were it not for the fact that the alcohol has slackened his facial muscles.

Fighting at parties normally takes place in the last quarter of the evening. If it takes place earlier than this, you invited the wrong people. The main cause is drunkenness, and the hardest part is getting the protagonist to back down without letting him feel he has lost face in front of his friends. Tell him that everything is fine if he stops now and goes no further.

Do not say:

'Well, thank you *very* much for the humiliating public exhibition. Now that you've embarrassed everyone in the room you might as well go home.'

Tact and calm are called for when dealing with rioting guests. Try taking his mind from the object of his anger by lightening the atmosphere.

Faced with a snorting, red faced, nine-foot tall hulk armed with a wine bottle, try these openers:

'Did you notice? Today it felt like spring is finally on the way.'

'I bet you can't guess who my top three favourite choreographers are.'

'What a great sweater! You *have* to tell me where you bought it!'

The reason your guests have resorted to fighting may just be that the party is on its last legs and needed livening up a little. In that case, you should know when to wrap things up for the evening before it ever reaches this stage:

13 FATAL SIGNS OF A DYING PARTY
~ ~ ~

1. You can see more than six square feet of unoccupied carpet in the lounge.

2. The numbers have cleared enough for you to be able to hear the music clearly.

3. More than four people are asleep.

4. Everyone is huddled in a corner with somebody except you.

5. The most lively room in the house is the kitchen, where people are making coffee.

6. Instead of lively party chatter, all you hear when the record ends is a deathly silence punctuated by the odd snore.

7. Someone is going through all the kitchen cupboards looking for marmalade.

8. The only two people left dancing are two Norwegian students whom nobody else seems to know.

9. Somebody asks if they can borrow a sleeping bag.

10. There are birds singing outside and you are suddenly aware that the room smells like a full ashtray.

11. The only person left from whom you can get any sensible conversation is the woman who is still waiting for the minicab she ordered three hours ago.

12. The only food left on the buffet table is a squashed slice of mushroom quiche with a smouldering Marlboro stuck in the top.

13. You catch yourself making a mental note to never, ever hold another party.

HOW TO WRECK SOMEONE ELSE'S PARTY

~ ~ ~

If you really hate the person throwing the party, you may just decide to have done with it and misbehave totally. This will ensure that (a) that person will never invite you again and (b) the other guests will have something to talk about for months to come.

The best way to wreck someone else's party is to become the centre of attention yourself. Try one of these attention grabbers:

1. Come dressed as a recently deceased and much-loved media personality.

2. Keep your Sony Walkman on all evening. Sing out loud.

3. Hand out 'candid' 8 × 10 glossies of the host/hostess in the shower.

4. Wear a dressy optional extra, i.e. a parrot.

5. Bring along someone famous and keep putting your arm round them. Leave early together.

6. Arrive bearing a Chinese takeaway.

7. If male, wear a smart suit and tie, and hide something enormous down your trousers.

8. Throw handfuls of money at people. Especially while they are eating.

9. Hand out invitations to a much more spectacular party which you are throwing next week.

10. Drunkenly challenge the host to a duel with loaves of garlic bread. Try to cut the tops off of the mantelpiece candles, like The Prisoner Of Zenda.

11. Drop a cufflink into the punchbowl and loudly rediscover it.

12. Throw a writhing-on-the-carpet epileptic fit which is pure 'Miracle Worker' by way of 'The Exorcist', and just as they are forcing a spoon between your teeth, stand up and announce that you were just joking.

13. Find out what the host/hostess will be wearing, and turn up in exactly the same clothes, but with cheap pricetags hanging from them.

14. Learn to throw your voice. During a quiet part of the evening, give the host bizarre gastric problems.

15. Bring a tiny puppy with you, inside your shirt, and keep showing it to women.

16. Get sick and voice your suspicions about the food.

17. Arrive in formal attire and announce that you can't stop, being on your way to a dinner party being thrown for Richard Gere, but that you *can* take two female guests with you.

15. The party quiz

The following quiz is designed to see if you have picked up any understanding so far of what parties entail and how you should behave when attending them.

SECTION 1. TRUE OR FALSE
≈ ≈ ≈

a. There is a government ministry in charge of party throwing called the Cocktail Cabinet.

| TRUE | | FALSE | |

b. The best way to attract a sexual partner at a party is to tell him/her that you are not wearing any underwear.

| TRUE | | FALSE | |

c. The best way of entertaining guests at dinner is to stick the end of a French loaf on your nose and do Jimmy Durante impersonations.

| TRUE | | FALSE | |

d. The only way you can get red wine out of an Irish lace tablecloth is with a lit match.

| TRUE | | FALSE | |

SECTION 2. MULTIPLE CHOICE
≈ ≈ ≈

a. <u>The main course at the dinner party is sweetbreads.</u> Do you:

1. Discreetly slide the contents of your dinner plate into your lap and later flush it all down the loo. ☐

2. Say: 'Sorry, but I don't eat things which look like

they belong in the close-up shots of a pornographic film.' ☐

3. Simulate eating and chewing, but save it in your mouth for disposal later. ☐

b. <u>The best excuse for leaving a party early is:</u>

1. 'I have to go home now because I'm really not enjoying myself here.' ☐
2. 'Well, I'm off. Your party and I are both tired.' ☐
3. 'I'd love to stay but "Dynasty" is on in twenty minutes.' ☐

c. <u>A daiquiri is:</u>

1. A cocktail. ☐
2. An old television show about a safari park. ☐
3. What used to be western Nigeria. ☐

SECTION 3. PARTY MANNERS
~ ~ ~

a. <u>The best way to get someone to refill your glass is to:</u>

1. Drain it noisily and set it upside down on the table with a bang. ☐
2. Clench the lower lip of the empty glass in your teeth and peer at your partner through the bottom, screwing up one eye. ☐
3. Roll up your sleeve and thrust your hand into the glass with a cry of, 'Nope, nothing in *here!*' ☐

b. <u>The best way to excuse yourself from a group of dull conversationalists is to:</u>

. . . subtly indicating that it's your round . . .

94

1. Faint and be carried out. ☐

2. Say: 'Won't you excuse me for a moment? I just spotted someone much more interesting.' ☐

3. Say: 'I'm going to the toilet. Can I get anyone a refill?' ☐

c. <u>The best way to change a conversation round to a topic you wish to discuss is to say:</u>

1. 'How fascinating. You must tell me more about it the next time Halley's comet passes the earth.' ☐

2. 'I agree with everything you say. But then I agree with anyone if it will shut them up.' ☐

3. 'Ha ha, yes, but enough about you, let's talk about me.' ☐

SECTION 4. HANDLING THE GUESTS
~ ~ ~

a. <u>Your stilted conversation with several guests just ground to a halt, and there seems little chance of reviving it. Do you say:</u>

1. 'I do impressions. Name any South African bird.' ☐

2. 'Has anyone else in this group actually killed someone?' ☐

3. 'I think deep down most women secretly want to be raped.' ☐

b. <u>Pick the odd item out from these party takealongables:</u>

1. Beaujolais. Chablis. Moët et Chandon. Sweet Spanish liqueur with plastic tree in bottle.

2. Cold quiche. Upside down cake. Profiteroles. Col. Sanders' family bucket.

How did you score?

SECTION 1. TRUE OR FALSE

If your answers are predominantly FALSE, consider yourself socially acceptable. If you marked all questions TRUE, consider yourself marginally less intelligent than your haircut.

SECTION 2. MULTIPLE CHOICE

The correct answer to each question is 1. If you failed to tick 1. at all, chances are your appearance at a society function is about as welcome as a French kiss at a family reunion.

SECTION 3. PARTY MANNERS

The correct answer here is 2. Any different answer indicates that you have the personality of a prawn cocktail, and pretty much the same appearance.

SECTION 4. HANDLING THE GUESTS

The last answer in each group is WRONG. To mark any of these indicates that you have the mind of something that hangs dripping upside down from a rock at low tide, are as interesting as the contents of someone else's nose, and possess about as much charm as a tramp's underpants.

16. Outdoor parties

HOW TO POUR TEA IN A RAINSTORM
~ ~ ~

Stay at home. In England, the concept of holding any sort of gathering in the open air is inviting the laws of nature to go on HOLD. Your decision to hold a party in your garden is an immediate signal for the TV weatherman to start sticking little pointy symbols all over his map. Yet fun may be had at outdoor gatherings like fetes, picnics, rock concerts and funerals.

Beach parties are best left to Annette Funicello and Frankie Avalon. How about a nice country picnic, the sort that the Famous Five used to have in Enid Blyton books?

WHAT TO TAKE TO A PICNIC PARTY
~ ~ ~

A reasonably equipped hamper (nothing too flashy, you're not the Earl of Brideshead).

Salt, pepper, mayo, ketchup, pickles, entire contents of fridge crisper.

Napkins left over from Christmas.

Nails for holding tablecloth to grass in Force 9 gale.

Party hats.

Food entirely pre-sliced, diced, tossed and slung between bits of bread.

Mineral water, car sick pills, sweaters, gumboots, raincoats, insect repellent, tent, WWII Russian Army Survival Kit, firelighters, fire extinguisher, penknife with attachment for getting boy scouts out of horses' hooves, Sunday newspapers which will blow all over field.

Stick for fending off irate farmer, in whose newly planted field you are sprawled.

Booze and glasses collected from garages.

Hairspray and comb for après party weather repair.

Assume that during the course of your meal, the wind will whip up to a speed unknown outside the island of Barbados during the rainy season, and that you will be sent chasing after butter wrappers which will be blasted all over the countryside until they come to rest in a field of bulls or on a farmer's face.

It is time to pack up and leave when the sleet is horizontal.

Remember that on a picnic all white clothes become white, green and brown clothes.

Be careful who you invite on your picnic.

Country people drone on about hedgeworts and the mating habits of bullfinches and the destruction of the countryside and National Heritage walks and the *Sunday Times* book of Things You Can Walk All Over.

City people moan about the grass being wet, refer to herds of cows as 'bunches', tell you they're freezing, complain that the air smells 'funny' and keep suggesting that you hold the picnic back in the car with the windows wound up and the heat full on. City women wear stiletto heels and thin silk blouses on picnics, and have to keep on the move to prevent sinking into the ground whenever they stop. City men wear nice Italian shoes which trek cowpats into the car.

The alternative to a picnic in the country is staying indoors to watch the Sunday afternoon movie, which is always either 'Rio Lobo' or 'The African Queen'.

If you don't wish to spend the afternoon wandering backwards and forwards across a meadow clutching a dripping paper bag full of teabags and eggshells looking for a litter bin, the alternative al fresco afternoon is available in the form of a nice village fete . . .

THE ORIGINAL FETE WORSE THAN DEATH
~ ~ ~

Anyone who thinks that village fetes exist only in Alan Ayckbourn comedies is obviously a city dweller. Fetes are a curiously English tradition, and are traditionally held on the first rainy Saturday of summer, coming replete with hearty vicars' wives, stout-legged women who sell inedible rock cakes, howling infants and exuberant scoutmasters. They are opened by a TV personality who used to be fairly popular ten years ago, and consist of everyone working their way round a field in a clockwise direction, stopping from time to time to buy home-made jams and have their fortunes read. If you are a 12-year-old kid, fetes are the most boring thing on the entire planet in the universe. After about an hour of this, the light drizzle turns into a torrential African thunderstorm and everyone heads for the tea tent. This, in the eyes of a child, is a definite upturn, as there is the remote possibility of seeing the vicar's wife, currently sheltering under a tree, get struck by lightning, or failing this, the family may decide to chuck the whole event and head homewards, in which case you can still get indoors before the start of 'Devil Invaders From Neptune' if you can keep Mum on the move past the shop windows between here and home.

The only other noticeably interesting thing about fetes is that parents, who until now have been entirely responsible adult human beings, suddenly start losing their children. The tannoys are thick with crackled details of kids without parents. Do they ever get claimed? What if two sets of parents both turn up claiming the same child? What happens to the ones that nobody comes for? Write your answer, in no less than fifty words, on a plain postcard and send it to me c/o the publisher.

GARDEN PARTIES
~ ~ ~

The idea here is that a lot of ladies in long white dresses traipse about somebody's lawn with platefuls of tiny sandwiches discussing modern art. Unlike fetes, these parties do not exist outside the British 'Swinging London' movies from the sixties, except in the sort of circles where the Right Hon. Lionel Boreham-Stiff marries a woman with a huge nose and bad teeth called Cynthia Sneek-Whining at the church of St Wetto the Chinless with a reception to be held in the modest 7,000 acre back garden of Lady Sneek-Whining RSVP do do try to come and bring 'Giggles' Dripcake and her husband 'Snotty' Spot-Poncer III who is something frightfully big in overseas investments.

Collectively such a garden party group looks pretty impressive in tiny *Tatler* photographs, with the exception of laughing young viscounts snapped with their eyes half shut as they slump against passing waitresses, but sadly their conversation reveals a group braincell-power which would fit comfortably on the point of a shooting stick.

These parties should not be confused with the new

wave of younger gentry disco bashes held at fashionable clubs and restaurants, which can be mildly diverting as long as you don't mind talking to people who prefer dogs to human beings.

UNUSUAL VENUES
~ ~ ~

But why follow the herd? There are no rules as to when and where you should have a party, with the possible exception of Never Throwing A Costume Ball In The Spare Bedroom. I've always wanted to have a party in a tent in the middle of the woods at midnight. Ideally, by myself.

THE REPTILE HOUSE PARTY
~ ~ ~

OK, no jokes about lounge lizards, this is serious. The reptile house at the London Zoo is a great place for a party. They rent out reception rooms, so that you may walk around ogling the salamanders while drunk. I attended a Christmas party there some years ago and found the idea of sharing a cocktail and a quip with a sloth infinitely preferable to consorting with the regular motley gaggle of guests. And you can introduce the animals to people.

'I'd like you to meet a friend of mine,' you say, tapping on the glass. 'This is my good friend Buddy Gecko.' Sorry, it's been a long day.

IMPROMPTU ZOO PARTY
~ ~ ~

Better than the Reptile House Party is your own private zoo party. I think this is probably frowned upon by the authorities, so if you know someone who works in a zoo, don't let them read this.

Lots of zoos have an area kept in darkness so that you can see nocturnal animals doing whatever it is they get up to at night, foraging for ants, copulating with their food containers and so on. The one in the London Zoo is called The Midnight World, and like most others it has a large enclosure filled with vampire bats. Here is where you arrange to meet your friends, by the vampire bat cage. Each of you brings something – red wine, paper cups, a few canapés perhaps, and you're all set to curl up beneath a thousand pairs of red eyes, to the accompanying flutter of leathery wings . . . At a time like this, ghost stories are in order. The occasional upward glance through the gloom at the sight of hundreds of hairy, fanged, rat-like creatures hanging upside down from branches by hooks chattering is enough to enhance any creepy tale.

Another good place for a spooky party is The London Dungeon, although if anything the venue succeeds too well by half. I attended a party there, and despite the fact that mulled wine was served to ward off the chill air, the idea of conducting whimsical party banter against a gibbet complete with rotting corpse was enough to drop most people into a profound melancholy for the remainder of the evening.

THE GRAVEYARD PARTY
~ ~ ~

How about a get-together in the park at midnight, you chaps? Better still, let's meet in the old cemetery! Ghost stories around glowing embers, the imprint of an ancient epitaph stamped back to front on your bottom from sitting on a tombstone, the sudden crack of a twig somewhere off to the left in the darkness of damp elms, the wraith-like figures of Burke and Hare emerging from the rolling ground mist, the burning desire to rid yourself of six pints of lager against Karl Marx's tomb . . . at midnight anything is possible!

FIREWORK PARTY
~ ~ ~

The first thing you need for a successful firework party is seventy woolly jumpers, because as soon as everyone gets outside to watch the display, the temperature plunges to below freezing. Guests find their fingers sticking to their wine glasses and ice ferns forming on their spectacles. At this point, hand everyone a jumper and point them towards the food, which should preferably be a spiced or curried dish, like chili or vindaloo. By serving food which will burn your guests' mouths, you will be allowing their facial muscles to thaw sporadically for the purpose of holding conversations.

The one common sense rule they never print in the firework safety code book is this: Light Your Fireworks Before You Get Drunk. There are a few sights more disturbing than spotting a swaying guest at the end of the garden clutching a gin and tonic in one hand and listening to a lit Atom Blaster by holding it flat against his ear with the other. Something else to watch for is Firework One-Upmanship, whereby each guest tries to bring a bigger, deadlier firework than the next, and you find yourself with a table full of enormous display explosives, the kind you

… clutching a drink in one hand and holding
a lit *Atom Blaster* against his head.

104

are supposed to bury three feet in the ground and light from behind a wall of sandbags.

It is important that you organise your fireworks early in the evening. No party must be allowed to become a bore, and you are risking this by asking your guests to hang around in the night air while you potter about at the other end of the garden with a safety light. Fireworks divide into five main categories.

1. TINY

This includes little rockets that simply drop off their sticks when you light them, sparklers, which are great if you don't mind your carpets showered with red hot shards of metal, and bangers so small they could be confused with the cat's suppositories.

2. SMALL

These all just spit gold sparks for eight seconds before dying. The same basic firework seems to be sold under 2,000 different names. Catherine Wheels which stop spinning moments after being lit are in this group. So are fiery little cones which give your eyes blind spots for the next twenty minutes.

3. MEDIUM

Rockets which go down next door's chimney, Roman Candles which rain blazing coloured balls on horrified guests, and bangers which leave your ears feeling as if they just attended an Iron Maiden concert are included here.

4. LARGE

Display fireworks that give the cat angina and the parrot palpitations, enormous striped tubes which you have to nail to posts, silver fountains that you have to watch through a piece of smoked glass and rockets that get mistaken for UFOs by nearby radar bases are amongst the heavy duty pyrotechnic items which will be causing terminal mange in your herbaceous border in the 'LARGE' firework group.

5. SILLY

This category is reserved for the marine flares your father brought along which are capable of melting through concrete, the huge bangers which you're supposed to notify the police about before firing, the military tattoo rocket which caused a woman passenger on a passing 747 to spray her gin and tonic over the window, and the display firework labelled 'STAND 120 YARDS BACK' which was inadvertently planted six feet away under a rose bush and blew a hundredweight of soil into the air, made everyone's faces black, sucked out the cat's eardrums and shattered every single pane of glass in the vicar's greenhouse over a quarter of a mile away.

Furthermore, be warned of the following . . .

THINGS TO BEWARE OF AT A FIREWORK PARTY
~ ~ ~
1. The man rummaging through the firework box with a lit cigarette in his mouth.

2. The two drunks who are deciding to settle their differences with lit Roman Candles.

3. The punk who asks you if you have any 'throwing bangers'.

4. The guy who walks backwards towards a fizzled firework as he reassures everyone that it has simply failed to light.

5. The budding science major who is sitting hunched over a pile of dismantled fireworks playing 'mix n' match'.

6. The practical joker who creeps around behind people, armed with Ariel Bombshells.

And finally, don't forget to check that the guy on top of the bonfire is just a heap of straw-stuffed clothes and not one of your sister's stoned boyfriends.

RIVERBOAT PARTIES
~   ~   ~

Now, of course, there is one thing wrong with riverboat parties, i.e. YOU CANNOT GET OFF. Avoid disco boats that go up and down the river all evening as they are invariably organised by the AWFUL DJ's from Chapter 5. During the course of a typical night on a riverboat, the following things can be counted upon to happen:

1. It will rain torrentially from the moment you climb on board.

2. Everyone will be freezing cold, even inside.

3. You will have enormous difficulty understanding the instructions for operating the toilet.

4. You will bang your head at least twice on low ceiling pipes.

5. All the girls with no one to dance with will sit in the single chairs lining the pointy end of the boat.

6. There will be a disgusting sign in the loo which reads 'DO NOT PUT ANYTHING DOWN THE TOILET WHICH YOU HAVE NOT FIRST EATEN'. Your reference to this sign will keep the conversation going later.

7. Someone will slip over on the wet deck above and really hurt himself.

8. The throbbing of the engine will make several party guests with delicate stomachs horribly sick.

9. The drink will run out ages before the boat gets back to the dock.

10. The boat will pass several beautiful landmarks which cannot be seen in the dark.

11. All women in high heels will be forced to spend most of the evening sitting down.

12. Everyone will run to the windows and wave each time a boat passes in the other direction.

13. Your sense of balance will be put to the test when you attempt to eat from a damp paper plate, standing up, while the boat hits the wake of a passing tug.

14. You – and everyone else – will, in the process of catching a cold, discover what landlubbers you really are.

THE GREAT SCAVENGER HUNT
~ ~ ~

Ever been on a Scavenger Hunt? No? Funny, nobody else seems to have been on one either. But I am here to tell you that there is no better way of simultaneously making friends and enemies while having a terrific time. For a good Scavenger Hunt you will require the following:

Between twenty and thirty friends, some of whom should be good drivers.

One car between every four or five people.

Pencils and paper.

Shopping bags.

Food and drink.

Here's how the evening goes:

1. As soon as your guests have all arrived, serve just one drink and a snack for them to become briefly acquainted with each other.

2. Divide the assembled group into teams. Each team must be able to squeeze into one car. Appoint the driver of each car as the team leader.

3. Provide a list of objects to be 'scavenged'. Each team must collect all the objects mentioned on your list. Fifteen items should be enough.

4. Set a maximum time limit of, say, two hours to collect everything on the list.

5. Arrange a reward for the winning team. Distribute the lists and provide pencils and paper for each team.

6. Wave everyone off and relax for a couple of hours. If you want to, you may elect to go along with one of the teams. Pick the team with the two most sexually attractive members and squeeze into the back of the car with them. Make the driver go around a lot of corners at high speeds.

A SAMPLE SCAVENGER LIST
≈ ≈ ≈

Scavenger hunts are much easier to organise in the USA because most stores stay open late, thus increasing the variety of items-to-be-scavenged that you can include on your list. Here in England you will have to tailor your list to suit the opening hours in your area, or hold your party during the day. You may decide to make your list risque and outrageous. You may prefer it to pass a number of watering holes along the route. The balance is up to you. Here are a few ideas for items to be collected:

A photograph of your team

The picture must clearly show all members of the team. It may be obtained from a station instant photograph booth.

A matchbook from a bar of dubious reputation

A strip club, perhaps, or dangerous waterfront hang-out. Pick somebody in the car who you don't like for this one. Watch to make sure they go in.

A matchbook from a heavy leather lesbian disco

Always a good one this. Send the same person in again. The trick to gaining admittance is in employing charm, wit and sexual allure to get past the bouncers. Remember, getting matchbooks or cocktail napkins from these places is easy if you're the first car arriving at the scene, but try facing an irate 700lb leather-clad gay biker who has had four separate carsful of people pulling the same stunt on him and you may need one hell of a lot of charm to get through this in one piece.

A kid's comic

Where to get one at 10 pm you ask? How about your house? Come on, you know you read them.

A beermat from at least one nice pub, bar or restaurant

You owe it to your guests to allow them a respite in comfortable surroundings at some point. The problem may be getting them out again.

An inflated balloon

Tough, until you remember that all night pharmacies are open, and if they don't exactly stock balloons, well, something will come to mind.

A baby picture of a team member

It's a stop-off at somebody's house. No cheating – it must be a genuine baby snap of a teamster. Babies do not all look alike. Ask your mother.

A silly hat

Extra points for extra silly hats, I think, don't you?

The signature of the doorman at The Ritz

Or similar plush hotel. No forging the name 'Stavros' in illegible scrawl, please.

A bus ticket

These can occasionally be bought without leaving the car, depending on the traffic flow and your ability to lean a long way out of a car window travelling at high speed.

Something shocking

The rules are pretty flexible on this one, but obviously the more shocking the better. And quite right too. Sex shops stay open late, or you may have something tucked away at home. You probably do if you bought this book.

A tracing from a tombstone

Who's going into the graveyard after dark? No, it's OK, I'll hang on in the car and wait. If you're not back in five, we're off.

A riddle clue

Use a book quotation or newspaper reference to disguise the nature of the object to be collected. This is an ideal item to end on.

Chinese (or other) takeaway food

You'll probably run into all the other teams on this, your final stop before returning to the host's house. Don't forget the soy sauce.

When all the teams have returned and the final reckoning is made, prizes can be awarded to the team with the most items, and perhaps a set of nasty forfeits for the losers . . .

You now have a household full of junk, by the way.

17. That's entertainment?

PARTY PERFORMERS
~ ~ ~

If you feel that your own vivacious personality will not be enough to hold the evening together, how about hiring an entertainer? The range available is none too inspiring, although you might conspire with friends to put on a show if you think your guests are that desperate for entertainment. Otherwise it's down to magicians, ecdysiasts (male and female), comedians, drag shows and fire eaters. There are problems with all these categories, needless to say, the main one being predictability.

THE PREDICTABLE MAGICIAN ACT
~ ~ ~

Coloured handkerchiefs which change order
Vanishing knot in bit of string
Three metal cups with vanishing foam balls
'Find the Ace' card trick which goes wrong
Chinese hoops with visible hinges
Ball floating on top of silk cloth
Wand into bunch of flowers
Dated jokey patter to cover dodgy sleight-of-hand
Posturing fat assistant in moulting sequined leotard

THE PREDICTABLE AUDIENCE REACTION
~ ~ ~

Cries of 'It's up your sleeve!' and 'It's got a false bottom!'

WITH ANY LUCK YOU MIGHT GET TO SEE:

Magician produce squashed, suffocated dove at Grand Finale.

THE PREDICTABLE STRIP ACT (FEMALE)

Appearance of well-proportioned woman with amazingly ugly face

Grinding pelvis to distorted heavy rock tape

Removal of bra by red-faced drunk in front row

Appearance of complicated fifties undergarments including nipple-caps with no visible means of support and suspender belt

Removal of red-faced drunk's spectacles which are then thrust down stripper's panties and returned steamed-over

Enormous buttocks resembling two wobbling muslin bags of cottage cheese

Unsuccessful opposite-direction tassle rotation

Baby oil breast massage in time to crackly Donna Summer record

THE PREDICTABLE AUDIENCE REACTION:

Assortment of sexist catcalls, embarrassed laughter, cries of 'Get 'em off', etc.

WITH ANY LUCK YOU MIGHT GET TO SEE:

Red-faced drunk becoming over-enthusiastic and getting his fingers broken by stripper's boxer boyfriend.

Removal of bra by red-faced drunk in front row.

115

THE PREDICTABLE STRIP ACT (MALE)
~ ~ ~
Appearance of sneaky faced boy who looks suspiciously like the one police found responsible for burglarising your house last summer

Removal of outer garments in time to Michael Jackson's 'Thriller'

Encouragement of females to stick pound coins down front of jockstrap

Grinding sexual motion meant to conjure up image of viewer coupling with performer after the show in return for jewellery

Forty-three miniscule permutations of underwear, each smaller than the last, like Russian dolls

Final disappointing non-appearance of much-promoted willy

THE PREDICTABLE AUDIENCE REACTION
~ ~ ~
Assortment of sexist catcalls, embarrassed laughter, cries of 'Get 'em off', etc.

WITH ANY LUCK YOU MIGHT GET TO SEE:
~ ~ ~
Surprise appearance of willy courtesy of over-constricting undergarment.

THE PREDICTABLE COMEDIAN
~ ~ ~
Mother-in-law jokes
Barmaid jokes
Complaint about lack of audience response
Handicapped people jokes

Joke about black people that goes too far

Complaint about black member of audience not being able to take a joke

Joke about nurse/stewardess/other with big breasts

Comment from comedian that anyone who doesn't find that funny must be a queer

Comment that he never has any trouble with these jokes in the rugby clubs

THE PREDICTABLE AUDIENCE REACTION
~ ~ ~

Dilemma of wanting to laugh at joke which was offensive but actually pretty funny.

WITH ANY LUCK YOU MIGHT GET TO SEE:
~ ~ ~

Comedian appear on TV talent show months later, where he gets less audience response than 10-year-old girl who plays the zither.

THE PREDICTABLE DRAG ACT
~ ~ ~

Overweight besequined man in corset miming to 'There's No Business Like Show Business'

Parade of foot-high nylon wigs and patent leather slingbacks in a Size 10

'Liza with a Z' Minelli impersonation which bears more resemblance to her mother

Artiste freezes midway through 'Everything's Coming Up Roses' when tape jams

Unevocative simulation of Barbra Streisand which nevertheless through years of repetition has been imbued with a Frankenstein-like life of its own

Rendition of Shirley Temple's 'On The Good Ship Lollipop' watched with the kind of emotion that occurs when faced with the sight of a 55-year-old man impersonating a 10-year-old girl

Rousing clapalong finale to current pop hit for which artiste has yet to master more than half the lyrics

Encore of Petula Clark's 'The Show Is Over Now' performed in threadbare boa and floor-length sequined dress bought through *Daily Sketch* special offer in 1956

THE PREDICTABLE AUDIENCE REACTION
~ ~ ~
Embarrassment of men, fascination of women.

WITH ANY LUCK YOU MIGHT GET TO SEE:
~ ~ ~
Quaking member of audience dragged on to stage and publicly humiliated.

THE PREDICTABLE FIRE-EATER
~ ~ ~
Five minutes taped overture heralds entry of emaciated man in black tights and girl who moonlights as magician's assistant

Banging together of swords and audience inspection of same

Swallowing of swords which (hopefully) is a sideshow trick

Drinking of combustible liquid and subsequent breathing of fire over ceiling tiles

Extinction of flaming sticks in mouth while assistant rummages around with rags and a bucket of paraffin

Running of flaming sticks over bare body which

explains performer's lack of chest hair

Spinning of flaming wheel in mouth with flaming swords in either hand to half-hearted applause from audience who have seen it done on TV

THE PREDICTABLE AUDIENCE REACTION
~ ~ ~

Nagging fear from people at the front that any minute now the ceiling will ignite into a fiery hail of melting polystyrene tiles.

WITH ANY LUCK YOU MIGHT GET TO SEE:
~ ~ ~

A slip-up in timing that results in an accident so horrendous that you will still be telling people about it in six months' time.

18. Functional dinners

In past centuries, thumbscrews, racks and bridles have been employed as torture devices on innocent victims. In the latter part of the twentieth century we have the functional dinner, an event rarely attended voluntarily, and one which has infinitely more painful effects. Functional dinners fall into three categories – the society function, the business function, and most sinister of all, the charity function.

Each type carries with it an insidious threat of blackmail that makes attendance compulsory. These evenings are laden with such intestine-gripping horror that enlistment in the territorial army would appear an attractive alternative.

If Heaven turns out to be a pleasantly appointed four-bedroomed house in the Thames Valley, and Limbo a doctor's waiting room filled with old copies of *Country Life*, then Hell must surely be a banqueting suite with luncheon buffet facilities for 2,000.

THE SOCIETY FUNCTION

~ ~ ~

Marginally less painful than the other two, but still a miserable experience for all concerned.

The Occasion:

A Bar Mitzvah, a wedding reception, the birthday celebration of a senior executive, a 'tribute' to a retiring boss.

The Venue:

Smaller ballroom or dining suite of a chain hotel, always to be found on the second floor of a Hilton or Holiday Inn, i.e. the Glastonbury Suite, the Disraeli Room, the 'Morocco' lounge, etc.

The Food:

The guest of honour's favourite dish, or rather a Big Hotel version of it, with the flavour taken out, so that if the meal is a Greek national dish, what arrives on your plate looks like a Pot Noodle with mincemeat dropped on top. Dessert is always lemon sorbet. Mercifully, you will have little time to devour this carbohydrate-riddled culinary sludge, because the entire meal will be punctuated with long and involved grace speeches offered up by an ancient padre/rabbi/other who is the oldest living friend of the guest of honour.

The Music:

Balalaika or Mariachi if ethnic. Big Hotel swing musicians playing clarinet versions of Neil Diamond songs in mauve lounge suits, intercut with violin waltzes to let the clarinet players get their breath back.

Moments to remember:

Being introduced to someone's gormless son/daughter by their mother, who thinks you may be able to help force the hapless child into a totally unsuitable career.

Being trapped into dancing with a woman whose icy indifference to being led around the dance-floor suggests that she modelled herself on Estelle in Great Expectations at a very early age.

Being forced to sing 'For He's A Jolly Good Fellow' or 'Auld Lang Syne' and finding that your crossed arms are linked with, on the left, a woman whose sweat glands seem concentrated entirely in the palms of her hands, and on the right, a waiter.

OUTCOME
~ ~ ~

Argument over bill centreing on the amount of wine drunk in the course of the evening which continues until two thirty in the morning and resolves itself in a compromise reached by the host buying the waiters large Chivas Regals.

THE BUSINESS FUNCTION
~ ~ ~

An event attended either because to stay away would be to suspend a question mark over the trajectory of your career, or because the invitation had been offered to everyone else in the building including the post-boys, and you were one of the few who at the time thought it might be fun to accept.

The Occasion:

Annual company get-together, awards ceremony, end-of-conference knees-up.

The Venue:

The larger ballroom or dining suite of a chain hotel, i.e. the Prince Albert Memorial Ballroom, the Madame Curie Dining Suite, the Lady Isobel Barnet Wing.

The Food:

Either the stand-in-line-for-three-quarters-of-an-hour-

*Slivers of pâté followed
by a tiny lump of dried-up steak.*

123

for-a-chicken-casserole-buffet, or the slivers-of-pâté-followed-by-a-tiny-lump-of-dried-up-steak-meal. Business dinners are generally regarded by the serving staff to be sado-masochistic affairs where grudges can be worked off against unsuspecting diners and wine can be hijacked homewards in unprecedented quantities.

If waiting for your meal becomes a bore, remember, there's probably enough food stuck to your silverware to constitute a starter.

The Music:

A band in blue velvet dinner jackets and polycotton dress shirts play disco hits revamped into a kind of big-band swing style most frequently heard in supermarkets while middle-aged company secretaries perform an old-English hotel folk dance resembling The Twist.

Moments to remember:

Sitting facing a line of depressed single women in evening dresses waiting to be asked to dance while the men sit at a separate table getting drunk.

Realising that there are at least 500 other weird-looking people working for your company, none of whom you were aware even existed before now. Suffering through an awards ceremony in which a stainless steel plaque is presented to an employee nobody likes by a board director everyone thought was dead.

Suffering through an acceptance speech following said awards ceremony in which the honoured employee takes time to thank everyone in his department by name, and pauses to tell a funny little story illustrating the character of each one.

OUTCOME
~ ~ ~

The secretaries get sick, the post-boys get drunk, and your department head eyes you stonily as you tipsily attempt to explain where you think he is going wrong in his handling of accounts.

THE CHARITY FUNCTION
~ ~ ~

An event hallmarked by the £50 ticket which you are pressured into buying by your immediate superior or by the fact that all your business rivals will be lending their support to the cause.

The Venue:

The Grand Ballroom of the hotel. For example, the Aga Khan Palace Suite, the Rudyard Kipling Memorial Hall, the Dame Edith Cavell State Room, etc.

The Occasion:

Help-Save-The-Blue-Nosed-Otter-In-High-Barnet Wildlife Fund, the Raise-A-Million-To-Build-A-Retired-Ballroom-Dancers-Home Society, the Help-Stamp-Out-Sciatica-In-Moorhens Club.

The Food:

Wholesome English grub – cockles to start with, steak and kidney pie, apple crumble and custard to follow. The amount of food on your plate is strictly disproportionate to the amount you have paid. Service throughout the meal will be surly if not non-existent, and at the end of it the only thing to have been taken away will be your breath.

The Music:

There probably isn't any. You're not here to enjoy yourself, you're here to listen to speeches about the coming extinction of the splay-footed throatwarbler, or the proposed new wing of the orphanage. This, incidentally, will be the only time in your life when the subject is mentioned. You will never find out whether the new wing was built or if indeed the last throatwarbler expired in a tubercular fit.

Moments to remember:

Function room hostesses inviting you to partake in a charity raffle in which the prizes are things like a pair of bedsocks knitted by the Countess of Northumberland. Participants are encouraged to write their signatures on the backs of notes, preferably the larger denominations, and drop them into a clear plastic bag – a clever device for making you look cheap if you drop in anything less than a tenner.

Also memorable: a very old star personality being introduced at the microphone to say a few words about 'a cause very close to my heart', 'giving generously' and 'no worthier reason for giving as much as one possibly can'. Star refers to piece of paper whenever it comes to the name of the charity.

OUTCOME:

~ ~ ~

You will leave with your boredom threshold broken

to a new limit and will head straight for the nearest takeaway pizza bar in the area. You will also leave with a considerably thinner wallet/purse/chequebook, feeling distinctly uncharitable. The thought of strangling a duck or an orphan will cross your mind more than once.

19. Sex at parties

'WHOOPS, SORRY, I WAS JUST LOOKING
FOR MY COAT.'

~ ~ ~

It would seem that a lot of parties take place solely for the purpose of introducing people to each other with a view to drunken coupling on the coats as soon as first-name terms are reached.

Oh, I know that never happens at your parties, but that's why they're so bor, er, so successful. That's because you don't ever invite the following people:

One divorced female neighbour in a leopardskin sweater who drinks gin cocktails faster than you can mix them and has a laugh like someone trying to start a Morris Oxford.

Two vampish air hostesses who lick their lips when they look at men and go to the toilet together to reapply their make-up three times an hour.

A bald, leering work associate whose idea of repartee is finding the double meaning in everything anyone says to him, then snorting with giggles.

A young male teacher whose ardent argument for feminist reform is undermined by the fact that he cannot remove his eyes from the breasts of the woman he is talking to.

Two foreign students whose mastery of the finer sexual points in the English language are just enough for them to get their lights punched out.

But Goodness, you don't want these people at your party. There are much more civilised ways of hunting out a possible partner. The English are the undisputed champions of the euphemism. The Americans may refer to beds as 'designer sleep furniture' but it takes the English to come up with 'bathroom stationery' as a polite term for toilet paper. Listen in on the conversation of your guests, and you might find a lot more going on than passing the cocktail nuts.

THE BRITISH WAY OF PARTY PROPOSITIONING
~ ~ ~

WHAT HE SAYS	WHAT HE MEANS
'That's a very pretty dress.'	'God, you have a terrific body.'
'That's a very unusual necklace.'	'I would like to press my nose into your cleavage.'
'I admire a woman with a career.'	'I'm bored talking about your job. Let's talk about your tits.'
'I've always been in favour of women's independence.'	'If I say what you want to hear, will it get me laid?'
'Why don't we go out on to the balcony? It's cooler out there.'	'I don't want my wife to see us.'
'Oh, you live in town? That's very convenient for work, isn't it?'	'I could stop off at your place after work for a quickie and be back home in time for "Hill Street Blues".'
'I'd be very happy to give you a lift home.'	'A lift home will cost you a grope in the car, minimum.'
'Here's my number. Give me a call some time.'	'Even though you turned me down, there's no way I'm going to look anything other than totally nonchalant about it.'
'You don't like dancing? Another time, perhaps.'	'Not interested? Rotten legs, anyway.'

129

WHAT SHE SAYS	WHAT SHE THINKS
'My dress? Why, thank you.'	'Eat your heart out, Baldy.'
'I'll just sit this one out, thanks anyway.'	'Dance with you? Are you *insane*?'
'Somebody's just getting me a drink, thanks.'	'Dig a hole and drop in, Fat Boy.'
'Oh, you're having a trial separation?'	'Oh, you're happily married?'
'Well, I'm busy for a few weeks, but after that, well . . .'	'The thought of being near you makes my skin crawl, but I'd like you to think there was still a chance . . .'
'I'm sure we'll bump into each other somewhere.'	'Give me a list of the places you frequent so I know where to avoid.'
'You went out with Elsa? She and I are old friends.'	'She told me you have the smallest penis she's ever seen, and she's seen a few.'

There's something about the atmosphere of a party which encourages people to lie, or at least, drop into character – for example, The Smoothie, The Wimp Who Needs Understanding, and so on. Just being yourself breaks through party conventions, and at least presents a refreshing attitude, although this does not wash at Californian parties, as the people you meet are so far removed from anything remotely connected with real life that they will just stare at you with their mouths open. This is because they are (a) trying to understand your accent and (b) aware that you are talking about something other than money, tanlines, diets or cocaine, in which case you might as well be having a conversation on the moon.

HOW TO TELL IF SOMEBODY AT A PARTY IS SEXUALLY ATTRACTED TO YOU
~ ~ ~
Wouldn't it help if people had little bells about their

heads that rang to let you know they were interested in you? Looks like God missed a trick there! You may think that the only sure way to find out is by asking millions of boring polite questions and sitting through hours of dull childhood anecdotes before getting down to the more intimate details. But no! There are sure tell-tale signs to let you know that the person sitting next to you with the gin and bitter lemon would happily drink your bathwater if you asked them.

For instance, watch for the woman who:

1. Stands leaning towards you with her right hand against the wall by your ear.

2. Stands listening to you and nodding as she picks bits of fluff from your jumper.

3. Looks at you from under heavy lids, breathes in deeply and pulls the bottom of her woolly down.

4. Leans across the table resting her chin on her knuckles and runs her tongue over her teeth.

5. Eats a cocktail sausage in a suggestive manner while you talk.

As for the men, watch for the ones who:

1. Uncross their legs and rearrange their underwear as they listen to you.

2. Blow bubbles into their pints as you walk past, and growl.

3. Bite their fists when they think you're not looking.

4. Lean across you to get a cigarette and force you into the back cushion of the sofa.

5. Give you a friendly pat on the knee, even though both of you are standing up.

These are the tell-tale signs of the more sexually aggressive people at your party. There are other, more reticent guests who could, if coaxed with subtlety and gentility, be persuaded, as in days of yore, that life can be more fulfilling with a partner who is tender and caring, who will walk them into the garden beneath the light of a thousand stars, and wait at least ten minutes before offering them a bunk-up in the begonias.

A WORD ABOUT PARTIES FULL OF BEAUTIFUL, LOVING, INTELLIGENT PEOPLE WHO MUTUALLY AGREE TO HAVE AN EXPERIMENTAL GUILT-FREE SEXUAL FREE-FOR-ALL WHERE EVERYONE CAN FEEL GREAT AND TALK ABOUT IT AFTERWARDS WITHOUT EMBARRASSMENT.

Forget it. There's no such thing.

MAKING THE FIRST MOVE
~ ~ ~

Many people would prefer to leap from a tall building than cross a room and ask someone if they'd like to dance. Me, for one. Why is it that we become such cowards at parties? What can be done? Well, a small, painful operation could remove the Shy Nodes from the back of your brain, thereby turning you into a gaudy, tasteless loudmouth – but does the world *need* another Liberace? Instead, try one of the following approaches:

1. Say something that the other person will *have* to agree with. For example:

'It's very warm in here, isn't it?'

(To be used when the temperature exceeds 100 degrees farenheit)

'Isn't your name Frances?'

(After you have ascertained the name by rifling through her handbag)

'Isn't Andrew Lloyd Webber living proof that all the money in the world can't make you attractive?'

2. Say something that will imbue the doe-eyed innocent you are addressing with a sense of total awe. For example:

'Hey, didn't I see you at Bruce Springsteen's party last week? I didn't stay long myself . . . I only went as a favour to Paul and Linda. Besides, if you stay too long at one gig, you upset Elton, although Madonna said that Boy George was annoyed at me leaving so soon.'

BEWARE of meeting anyone who uses the following . . .

DREADFUL CREEPY AWFUL TURN-OFF LINES

1. 'Hey! Smile! It's not that bad!'

2. 'You remind me of someone I used to go out with.'

3. 'Haven't I seen you somewhere before – NO – Don't tell me . . .'

4. 'I bet you're a Virgo. Ask me why I say that.'

5. 'You're a stewardess, right?'

6. 'I bet I can guess your name. You look like a Susan.'

7. 'Boy, you look really fed up.'

8. 'I bet you used to be a model with those legs.'

9. 'Are you in television? No? You amaze me!'

10. 'Can I get you a drink? *Why not?*'

Worse than all of these come-on lines put together is the 'lifestyle dialogue' opening conversation of Medallion Man. Who is Medallion Man? Why, he's the guy who, even at this moment is shambling across the room to the young girl standing alone on the other side of the room. And he's as instantly recognisable as a nun in a pool hall.

HOW TO SPOT MEDALLION MAN
~   ~   ~

1. He has three gold chains around his neck, one dangling a gold plated penny, another with his birth symbol and a third with his initials.

2. His shirt is open almost to the waist. He sports his chest hair as if it were a status symbol, and possesses an ego you couldn't dent with a rotary chainsaw.

3. He wears bronzer, hair spray and enough Eau Sauvage to kill a small animal.

4. He is holding in his stomach, but occasionally forgets and lets it out when he thinks he's unobserved. His metal belt buckle could get cable TV.

5. He is wearing a digital watch with calculator and built-in alarm which keeps going off, a gold identity bracelet and two rings made from rock-like chunks of gold.

6. He is wearing white patent leather shoes with tassels.

7. His hairstyle consists of either (a) a raft of crinkly hair lying across the bald spot, looking as if it was arranged in place by a trap-door spider or (b) grey sideburns and a chestnut brown wig.

WHAT MEDALLION MAN WILL SAY

~ ~ ~

'Hey hey hey little lady (Chucks her under chin) cheer up life's not that bad, wow did anyone tell you you have an amazing body, no really I know a lot of cute girls but you are really something, do you go to Floozies cocktail bar, I think I've seen you in there I'd remember those legs anywhere, look I don't want you to think this is a come-on but I feel there could be something good between you and me, you know? (Places hand in small of girl's back and slides it down) My (Porsche, TR7, Jeep, company hatchback) is parked right outside, what say we go back to my place and (listen to my new digital sound system, watch porno videotapes) and really get to know each other (Girl walks off, revolted at prospect) Hey! Hey! What'd I say? (Under breath) Bitch.'

It's odd that you'll always catch Medallion Man at parties looking for a perfect 10, unaware that he himself rates a Minus 2. But enough about him. This chapter is about sex at parties, and that's one thing Medallion Man never gets.

ACTUALLY DOING IT

~ ~ ~

It is not polite to have sex at other people's parties. When you go shopping, you don't start eating the groceries in the street, do you? Well then, wait until you get home, or have a snack in the car to keep you going. Looking for a bedroom to have sex in is NOT ON. If you really cannot wait, or your partner only has hours to live, or they've just sounded the four minute warning, use the

135

'I bet you're a Virgo.
Ask me why I say that.'

airing cupboard. It's nice and warm, and there are towels. DO NOT use the kids' bedroom, as it is an enormous sexual turn-off attempting foreplay on a four-foot long bed shaped like an aeroplane. It is also impossible to return to the party afterwards without looking like you just had sex. There's something about a man with his shirt tucked visibly into the waistband of his underpants that gives the game away.

ORGIES
~ ~ ~

I know, you thought you'd find a juicy chapter here about suburban couples throwing their car keys into the middle of the coffee table, and the revealed secrets of the Barnet Bondage and Discipline Coffee Mornings. Well, you're not, because I happen to find the whole subject distasteful, and furthermore, in keeping with Queen Victoria's views on lesbianism, I don't think they exist in England. The weather is too cold, and most English people look extremely unappetising in their underwear.

20. Jet set parties

You see them at gallery openings and movie premieres, book launches and charity drives, the so-called 'glitterati', frosty smiles frozen in the flashes of photographs, arms around each other, laughing and hugging. But what are these parties really like? What do the people who attend them find to talk about? And how do they get chosen to attend such occasions?

Well, to begin with there's a Celebrity Guest List – a list of all those people whose faces are currently in the newspapers and magazines. In fact, there are two lists. Those who you'd love to attend, and those who will actually turn up on the night.

THE CELEBRITY GUEST LIST
~ ~ ~

Desired Guest:	_Who you get instead:_
Michael Caine	Roger Moore
Madonna	Samantha Fox
Anthony Burgess	Stephen King
Ann Margret	Britt Ekland
Britt Ekland	Pia Zadora
Pia Zadora	Lassie
Stephen Sondheim	Andrew Lloyd Webber
Michael Jackson	Sacha Distel
Germaine Greer	Mary Whitehouse
Barbra Streisand	Dorothy Squires
Steven Spielberg	Michael Winner
Wham!	Brian Poole and the Tremeloes

Edward Kennedy
Bob Hope
Bruce Springsteen

Arthur Scargill
Bruce Forsyth
Shakin' Stevens

INTERNATIONAL JET SETTING:
AN AT-A-GLANCE TABLE OF PARTY TYPES
≈ ≈ ≈

COUNTRY	VENUE	PEOPLE	CONVERSATION
Paris	Montmartre studio, Prêt-À-Porter show in cafe.	Artists, models, fashion designers, food critics.	Sex, painting, fashion, food and sex.
Rome	Terracotta balcony above city, Frascati villa.	Fashion designers, crooked art dealers, film makers, models.	Women, fashion, money, sex, shoes.
USA (New York)	Minimalist hi-tech downtown loft, converted grain silo.	Writers, producers, models, hairdressers, actors, actresses, whiz-kid computer company heads.	Hair, clothes, name-dropping, deals, nightclubs, drugs, analysts, promotion, money.
USA (Los Angeles)	Poolside patio on Mulholland.	Actors (all currently working as waiters at Joe Allens) agents, lawyers, producers, studio execs, hairdressers, drug dealers.	Production problems, drugs, EST, studio politics, ex-lovers, rewrites, money, divorce, favourite sushi bars, where to have your poodle clipped, tanlines, drugs.
London	Damp-smelling house in Hampstead full of boring dun-coloured oil paintings.	Restaurant owners, media stars, foreign financiers, eccentric old people who don't do anything, lady novelists, elderly theatricals, elegant homosexuals in white socks.	The weather, house-hunting, wok cookery, difficulty of parking in the West End, books, outrageous price of Glyndebourne tickets, non-availability of baby-sitters, Booker prize shortlistings, difficulty of getting drains unblocked on public holidays, finding a laundry which will starch a shirt properly, playwrights who have 'gone off a bit' just lately, cricket, possibility of nuclear war, unions, TV shows, latest tabloid scandal, hats, cats, bats, gnats, etc, etc, etc . . .

All of which goes to prove that the British will discuss anything for any length of time providing they have a free drink in one hand.

HOW TO BEHAVE AT A JET SET PARTY
~ ~ ~

When attending a party filled with smart, wealthy people – and I am assuming here that you have genuinely been invited, and have not been sent an invitation by mistake – it is essential that you appear as smart and as wealthy as those around you. You must fit in. This can be achieved by following the do's and don't's listed below:

1. Do not forget to remove your cycle clips before entering room.

2. Do not wipe your nose on the back of your hand.

3. Do not 'put one behind your ear for later' when someone offers you a cigarette.

4. Do not hail waiters by placing two fingers between your teeth and whistling.

5. Do not demand brown sauce for your canapés.

6. Do not ask what time the last buses run.

7. Do smile evasively and change the subject when someone asks you what you do for a living.

8. Do stand near people discussing stock investments and shake your head, tutting as if you consider it a poor business risk.

9. Do arrive with your hair in curlers, explaining that you are going out after the party.

10. Do cover your face when someone takes a photograph.

11. Do leave early. Tell the host that you'd love to stay longer but that you are 'on a tight schedule'.

... forgot to remove his cycle clips
before entering the room.

141

12. Do say goodbye by kissing people on both cheeks with a loud 'MMMM', being careful not to actually touch them or show any real affection.

21. The perfect party

What if everything worked out fine? Given a chance to build an ideal set of circumstances around the event, what would you choose for your party? Well, in an ideal world, perhaps some of the following . . .

1. A house with a wet bar and a glass wall overlooking a lake.

2. Fifty guests whose fame as raconteurs, free thinkers, wits and movie stars is exceeded only by their modesty and desire to have a good time.

3. Music mixed by the DJs from Limelight in New York.

4. Beethoven as a next door neighbour.

5. A guest who is a scientist, and he's just invented this completely harmless drug that makes you feel incredibly happy, and instead of having bad side effects it actually supplies you with the day's intake of Riboflavin and Vitamin C, and it's really cheap to produce and he has some on him.

6. Vic, the barman from the Savoy, mixing the drinks.

7. Ella and Frank agreeing to run through a few old Porter numbers while Barbra goes to the loo.

8. Dino De Laurentiis popping over from his LA deli with a casserole dish under a teatowel.

9. A standing ovation from the guests as the Beluga caviar is brought in on the ice swan.

10. Barry Manilow accidentally locked in the cloakroom all evening.

THE WORLD'S WORST PARTY

~ ~ ~

As the evening wears on and on and on, you may find the entire event unstoppably slipping into the realm of something weird and awful. You know what you'll find at the world's worst party, don't you?

1. On your way into the room, the hostess will accidentally shut your fingers in the crack of the door.

2. When your best friend tries to stop a drunk from punching your bank manager's wife, he'll get a pint mug broken over his head.

3. All the people who get violently sick will agree that there's something 'off' in the ravioli dish you brought with you.

4. You will upturn a plate of barbecued ribs into your lap. Twice.

5. At dinner you will be seated between Mary Whitehouse and Arthur Scargill.

6. Your one contribution to breaking the silences between the sporadic, desperate conversation will be an appalling case of flatulence.

7. The woman who lost a crown against the toilet after slipping on your highly polished linoleum floor is a lawyer and plans to sue you.

8. Everyone stops dancing and the lights are turned up while you all look for a contact lens in the shag pile carpeting.

... everyone looks for a contact lens
in the shag pile carpeting.

145

9. You will finally agree to your neighbour's demand to turn the music down after he throws the side mirrors from your car through your greenhouse roof.

10. Barry Manilow will get the cloakroom door unstuck.

22. After the bomb

APRÈS-PARTY-THROWING FEARS

~   ~   ~

If you feel concerned about what unpleasant discoveries the dawn will bring following a particularly hectic bash, you are justifiably worried. Our research has proven that at least three of the following nasty surprises lie waiting for you. To be aware of these in advance is to be able to forestall them, but there are some high-risk elements in your house which you can do little to guard against.

Cigarettes are the biggest single menace. Coupled with the effects of alcohol, the average filter tipped Virginia Slim becomes a fiery torch of destruction. Here are a few more things to worry about:

1. Your brand new mustard yellow throw rug has received a fake leopard-skin effect thanks to your guests flagrant disregard of ashtrays.

2. For weeks after, you will have trouble flushing your toilet properly. You can solve the problem now by removing the cistern lid and taking out the chicken leg somebody dropped in there which is jamming your ballcock. (What kind of people did you invite, for God's sake?)

3. It can now be seen that you were robbed in your purchase of the three-piece lounge suite, which is not interior sprung at all but foam filled. It can be seen, because thanks to our old friend Mr Cigarette we can see in through the many burn holes on the arms of the couch, through which extrude hundreds of irregular shaped pieces of orange foam.

4. The kitchen counter is fringed with black marks indicative of ignored ciggies which have been lit and then left to their own devices. Speaking of the counter there is a jumbo-sized bottle of Coke stuck to it, which will prove slightly harder to remove than Excalibur from the stone.

5. Over at your beloved record collection we find forty empty sleeves and inner sleeves, and a great stack of unprotected records separated from each other by cheese and onion crisps. Your copy of the legendary 'missing' Stephen Sondheim 1972 live concert double album is filled with country pâté and huge scratchy flakes of buttered French bread.

6. Someone has trodden smoked salmon into the stair carpet, so be careful when descending with a tray of dirty wine glasses. Very slippy, is smoked salmon.

7. The tropical fish look decidedly peaky, possibly because their water tastes of gin and tonic. Someone decided to feed them last night too, but they don't seem to like pickled onions.

8. There are wine glasses and paper plates in the bathroom – enough to suggest that an entirely separate party seems to have been successfully held there.

9. There is an elastic-sided shoe in the refrigerator. Don't even ask.

10. Your cat, once the most gregarious of creatures, will no longer allow a human being within ten feet of it. Ever since the traumatic experience it suffered locked in

... *spends its days hiding beneath*
the couch hissing at anything that moves.

the spare room with a couple of drunken party guests, it has taken to spending its days hiding underneath the couch hissing at anything that moves.

11. Apparently somebody cooked and ate a whole leg of lamb – your lunch for tomorrow. A friend says it was the same person who spent the entire evening criticising the party until the drink ran out, whereupon he departed, pausing only to urinate in the azalias and toss his wine glass into the hedge.

12. Two weeks after the party, you find a mummified half-eaten salad on a paper plate down the back of the radiator. The cat would have found it before you, only it's still under the couch.

13. If you didn't know better, you'd *swear* that someone had been through your wardrobe, but people don't do that sort of thing at parties, do they? The next time you are in a rush to go to dinner and decide to wear an item of clothing unworn for a while, you will find a half-eaten stick of celery hanging out of the jacket top pocket.

14. The deep score-lines filled with white powder on your onyx coffee table, plus the ashtray filled with roaches indicate that your straight-laced neighbour and his wife (both of whom seemed very animated all evening) aren't quite as straightlaced as you thought.

15. The woman who works for 'Greenpeace' backed her jeep over your flowerbed when she left.

THE FOLLOWING ITEMS WERE LEFT BEHIND BY YOUR PARTY GUESTS

~ ~ ~

1. The shoe in the fridge (yes, yes, we know about that).

2. (Costume party) One of Cleopatra's breastplates, under the sofa with the cat. You used it as a saucepan lid for a week before realising what it was.

3. The jolly woman who works for 'Save The Whales' forgot her cycle clips.

4. A bright yellow Fair Isle sweater with red bobbles on it. Nobody who came to the party is prepared to admit ownership of it. Next week it will become a car waxer.

5. A grey scarf. There's *always* a grey scarf left behind after a party.

6. The pantyhose hanging from the upper bathroom window indicates that your teenage son's party wasn't quite the teddy bears' picnic you believed it to be.

7. Hairslides, chewing gum under the dresser and a pair of banana-flavoured edible panties (half eaten) indicate that your son may be considerably more sexually advanced than you ever were (or indeed are).

8. A set of upper dentures found on the buffet table may be taken as a veiled comment on the coarseness of your home-made country pâté.

9. A hat. Who on earth wears a hat? Nobody *you* know.

10. (Costume party) There's this *thing*. It's long and sprayed gold, with a wiggly thing on the end that goes around and . . . there's velcro along one side to stick it to something. It looks important and presumably somebody's costume is incomplete without it. In the bin.

11. Several bottles of unheard of wine from faraway countries. None of these are faintly drinkable. They never get opened, they just get passed from party to party. Many of them are years old. You will take them to the next few parties you go to and eventually they will return to the people who brought them in the first place, so that no one will ever discover what Norwegian claret tastes like.

12. A person. He's not anyone you've ever met before and he doesn't speak English very well. He looks like an exchange student, and you found him asleep upstairs, wrapped in a curtain. He doesn't seem in a hurry to leave, either, which is a worry.

'LET'S MISBEHAVE!'

WHAT PEOPLE WILL DO IN YOUR HOME
~ ~ ~

It can be safely assumed that if you take a normally polite, charming, neat, shy person and place him or her in a party environment, that person is likely in the course of the evening, to:

1. Be sick.
2. Become abusive.
3. Get violent.
4. Cry.
5. Break something valuable.
6. Embarrass you.
7. Steal.
8. Miss the bowl.

9. Hit your car.

10. Badmouth your party afterwards.

In my research I have been unable to discover what exactly triggers this dark side in the typical party guest, or who will be the most affected by the heady combination of alcohol, sexual innuendo and the devil's music.

I have a friend who unfailingly throws up every time he attends a party at my house. I tell him it's appallingly bad mannered. He tells me it's the barbecue sauce.

Broken items after a party usually include the toilet, which will never flush properly again, pictures knocked from walls, the stereo, which will remove its playing arm from records before they have finished for the rest of its life, glasses and plates, the cat, which now has a split personality and spends its nights in the attic making a noise like a baby, the chair that belonged to your grandmother, and every single one of your cassettes.

The people who break these things are the same people who tell everyone that your party was a hopeless bore. But what are their parties like? Ah ha, there's the catch, because they never hold parties – at least, if they do, you've never been invited.

So what is the answer?

Simply that you must expect to find a little damage if the party you are throwing is big and boisterous. If your Joan Crawford cleanliness complex is that serious, then keep the numbers down or just invite the catatonic ward of your local hospital. A nice party will be a very special treat for these incredibly handicapped people, who will be eternally grateful for an invitation to spend a day away from doing huge jigsaws and making hats out of cereal packets.

THE FINAL TALLY – WAS IT WORTH THE EFFORT?
~   ~   ~

If it was a party that somebody else threw, are you glad you went?

If it was a party that you threw, are you glad you went?

Before you decide, remember how you felt the next morning. And in the following Final Tally, award yourself 10 POINTS for every question you answer YES.

PARTY SUCCESS CHART
~   ~   ~

1. Did everyone leave with a better opinion of you than they had when they arrived?

YES ☐   NO ☐

2. Did the booze outlast the guests?

YES ☐   NO ☐

3. Did you take the chilli con carne off the buffet table before it grew cold and scabbed over?

YES ☐   NO ☐

4. Did you talk your cousin Daphne out of killing herself in the bathroom?
(No points if she killed herself somewhere else)

YES ☐   NO ☐

154

5. Did you succeed in convincing anyone that you possess qualities you know you don't have?
(Score double for convincing bank manager)

YES ☐ NO ☐

6. Did you appear sexually alluring, even after you'd finished dancing?

YES ☐ NO ☐

7. Did people look sincere when they thanked you for a fabulous evening?

YES ☐ NO ☐

8. Did you push guests to the front door rather than having to beg them to stay?

YES ☐ NO ☐

9. Were you able to forgive the smokers who used your ficus as an ashtray?

YES ☐ NO ☐

10. Are you prepared to do it all over again next weekend?

YES ☐ NO ☐

<u>100 POINTS</u> 'I Suppose I Just Love People.'

<u>50 PLUS POINTS</u> 'I Love People But That Woman Will Never Be Allowed In This House Again.'

<u>20 TO 50 POINTS</u> 'I Am Serving Sardines At My Next Party.'

<u>LESS THAN 20 POINTS</u> 'I Am Planning To Lock Myself In The Attic With Eight Records And A Lifetime's Supply Of Tinned Food Until The Year 2000.'

12 GOOD REASONS FOR GOING STRAIGHT BACK TO BED THE NEXT MORNING
≈ ≈ ≈

1. The first sight that greets you when you arise is a glass of Scotch by the side of the bed containing a cigarette butt, an olive and half a Ritz cracker.

2. When you look out of the window the first thing you notice is that your peach tree is full of waving cocktail sausages.

3. The state of your bathroom basin suggests that its last user was ill advised to consume a Chinese meal before arriving at your party.

4. Your face in the mirror, with its white tongue, red nose and eyes set in a chalky-hued face, resembles an archery target.

5. You are hit with a wave of nausea while emptying a pot of mayonnaise filled with cigarette ends.

6. When you pull back the curtains, the sudden surge of dazzling daylight causes your irises to slam shut audibly, and you feel like cowering in a corner, Dracula-style.

7. The singing of the birds in your garden makes you wish you owned a pellet gun.

8. Your mouth tastes as if you have been chewing a ball of dried glue all night, and your breath is as fresh as an airline toilet after a hijack.

9. The sight of your lounge makes you feel as if the four minute warning came and went last night without you noticing it.

10. The condition of your carpets suggests that the

Dancing Horses of Vienna were among last night's party guests.

11. The exchange student is still in the kitchen wrapped in a bedspread making toast.

12. The problem of how to remove confetti and Silly String from your shag carpets is too much for your mind to cope with this morning, and maybe ever.

Gentle Reader,

Thank you for coming to
The Ultimate Party
Book. We hope you had
a lovely time.

Please come again soon.
Or invite us to your
party. Address your
invitation to our
publisher. We look
forward to having fun
in your home.

CHRISTOPHER FOWLER
~ ~ ~
STUART BUCKLEY